GUITAR *signature licks*

Best of
Southern
ROCK

CONTENTS

ISBN 0-634-01989-9

HAL•LEONARD®
CORPORATION
7777 W. BLUEMOUND RD. P.O. BOX 13819 MILWAUKEE, WI 53213

Visit Hal Leonard Online at
www.halleonard.com

INTRODUCTION

The seventies are sometimes seen as a musical letdown after the glorious creative flowering of the counterculture sixties—somewhat of a sensory hangover, if you will. While not exhibiting the revolutionary breakthroughs wrought by legends like Jimi Hendrix, Cream, the Who, the Rolling Stones, and the Beatles, the era nonetheless produced a cornucopia of magnificent guitar-powered rock. Without question, some of the most spectacular instrumental extravaganzas came out of the Southern rock genre.

The deep roots of the genre can literally be traced back to the Western Swing music of the late thirties and forties by such bands as Bob Wills and the Texas Playboys. Though Wills sang and fiddled up front, the twin guitars of steel man Leon McAuliffe and electric guitar picker Eldon Shamblin were arranged to play harmony lines thirty years before the Allman Brothers Band. It would be the "Brothers," however, who brought the power of rock to the form through the soaring guitars of Duane "Sky Dog" Allman and Richard "Dickey" Betts beginning in 1969. Drawing on their monster blues chops and finely honed melodic sense (acquired partly through their genuine interest in jazz), they took the art of the jam to previously unknown heights. Blind Willie McTell's "Statesboro Blues" from *Live at the Fillmore East* set a standard for southern-fried blues, especially with Duane's stunning slide work, not yet surpassed. "Melissa" presented them in a laid-back setting with folky acoustic guitars supplying the underpinning for sweet diatonic electric musings in the coda, while "Ramblin' Man," the lyrical guitar showcase from the post-Duane era, gave overqualified former second guitarist Dickey Betts a chance to strut his stuff.

Lynyrd Skynyrd and the Marshall Tucker Band in the early seventies eagerly followed in the outsized footsteps of the ABB, each amassing a substantial audience. "Call Me the Breeze," by the cultish songwriter J.J. Cale, was an atypical but favorite cover by the triple-guitar heavyweight Skynyrd band, while "Can't You See" revealed the pop hit potential of the jazzy Tuckers. Meanwhile, a virtual Confederate Army of southern rockers brandishing six-string artillery had formed throughout the territory below the Mason-Dixon Line. Wet Willie, with their funky R&B influences, displayed regional pride with "Dixie Rock." Black Oak Arkansas, led by the hormonally overloaded singer Jim "Dandy" Mangrum, covered LaVern Baker's "Jim Dandy (to the Rescue)" along with flashing their own brand of raunchy boogie rock. Lead singer Donnie Van Zant, brother of Skynyrd's Ronnie, kept .38 Special going longer than most, scoring a pop hit with "Caught Up in You" in 1982. Molly Hatchet, with three guitarists led by Dave Hlubek, flirted with heavy metal and produced the aptly titled "Flirting with Disaster." Taking the triple-threat idea to the limit, the Outlaws "out-Freebirded" Lynyrd Skynyrd with the epic "Green Grass and High Tides." Carrying the "Stars and Bars" to a different beat was the Atlanta Rhythm Section, whose "So Into You" demonstrated an example of the mellow, easy-listening, jazzy song of the South.

Besides the cadre of good ol' boys who operated in the aura surrounding the Allman Brothers, there existed a number of groups from more diverse backgrounds and geographical locations who related stylistically. Delaney & Bonnie went from being an obscure blues and country act in the sixties to forming a traveling road show with various American and English "friends" like George Harrison. Eric Clapton joined them briefly after fleeing Blind Faith and provided the hot licks for "Coming Home." Creedence Clearwater Revival, from the other "South" (California), were virtual hit single makers in the late sixties and early seventies. Their extended, psychedelic version of Dale Hawkins' "Susie-Q" was a showcase for leader John Fogerty. The great state of Texas contributed a wild, live cover of Little Walter's "Thunderbird" to the genre via the hard-rocking, bluesy ZZ Top, featuring guitar virtuoso Billy Gibbons. Furthest afield was Mountain, named for big Leslie West from Long Island, New York, who's raucous "Mississippi Queen" betrayed British influences derived from "Slowhand" Clapton.

CALL ME THE BREEZE

Words and Music by John Cale
Performed by Lynyrd Skynyrd on *Second Helping* in 1974

Lynyrd Skynyrd's 1973 debut album flew in the face of convention with "Freebird," an epic guitar orgy, as the recording's centerpiece. At a time when sensitive singer-songwriters were beginning to rule the airwaves with short, personal musical statements, the rowdy guys from Jacksonville, Florida were wailing away for all they were worth. "Freebird" helped provide the Skynyrds with a measure of success that carried over to their sophomore effort, *Second Helping*. In addition to hits like "Sweet Home Alabama," "Don't Ask Me No Questions," and "Working for MCA," the album included a finger-snapping version of J.J. Cale's "Call Me the Breeze" that would prove popular enough to be re-recorded in alternate live versions on later releases. Not surprisingly for Skynyrd and singer Ronnie Van Zant, the lyrics deal with the freedom to leave a situation in a burst of romantic wanderlust.

"Call Me the Breeze" is a twenty-four-measure boogie blues with three distinct guitar parts arranged to form a rich panoply of complementary I–IV–V tonalities. Though Lynyrd Skynyrd have often been described as combining heavy British hard-rock tone with a Southern sensibility, here they call up a bright, crackly sound in keeping with the buoyant groove.

Figure 1–Verse 1

Verse 1 contains the basic harmonic elements of "Call Me the Breeze." Gtr. 2 (Rhy. Fig. 1A) plays barre chord boogie patterns with 5ths, 6ths, and ♭7ths appropriate to each chord change except for measures 12 (C♯5, C5, and B5) with 5ths, and measures 17–18 where open-string patterns are employed for the V chord (E). Though the forms themselves are regular and repetitive, the rhythmic variations breathe life into the accompaniment. Instead of being identical one-measure patterns throughout, the I chord (A) is arranged into four-measure increments that appear in measures 1–4, 5–8, and 21–24.

In contrast, Gtr. 1 (Rhy. Fig. 1) works in four-measure phrases that are rhythmically identical in the first two measures, but offer slight variations in the last two measures of each increment. Harmonically, the open position of A, combined with the F♯ relative minor pentatonic scale, is used for the I chord. The partial barre for the A at fret 2 is then moved up the neck in a parallel fashion for the IV (D) chord, and an open-position E chord is accessed for the V change.

Fig. 1

Moderately fast ♩ = 192

*A5

1. Call me the breeze;_ I keep blow - in' down_ the road._

Gtr. 2 — Rhy. Fig. 1A — *mf* — w/ slight dist.

Gtr. 1 — Rhy. Fig. 1 — w/ slight dist.

* Chord symbols reflect basic harmony.

Well, now, they

call   me   the breeze;   I keep blow - in'   down   the road.

Figure 2–First 24 measures of Guitar Solo

As Gtrs. 1 and 2 continue to provide a snappy rhythmic and harmonic bed, Gtr. 4 plays the blues. In measures 1–8 (I), the A7 triple stop popularized by Robert Johnson and Muddy Waters (among others) is picked sparsely like a broken chord. Building the tension, Gtr. 4 starts introducing triplets in measure 5 in a manner that evolves into a pile-driving rhythm in measures 7 and 8. In the remaining sixteen measures, the A composite blues scale in the root and extended positions is used to navigate the changes. Note particularly the tangy double-string bends in measures 13–16 (I) that includes the true "blue note" between the ♭3rd (C) and major 3rd (C♯). Combined with the E/C dyad, the ensuing tension begs to be released to the root (A) note that follows. In addition, the very hip repeating pattern of D–C–E–G that begins in measure 16 (I) and continues over the V (E), IV (D), and I chords through to measure 21 jacks up the energy level until it soars off the chart. In measures 23 and 24, the root (A) note, surrounded by the melodic F♯ (6th), B (9th), and C♯ (3rd) scale degrees, provides resolution while building momentum in the higher register.

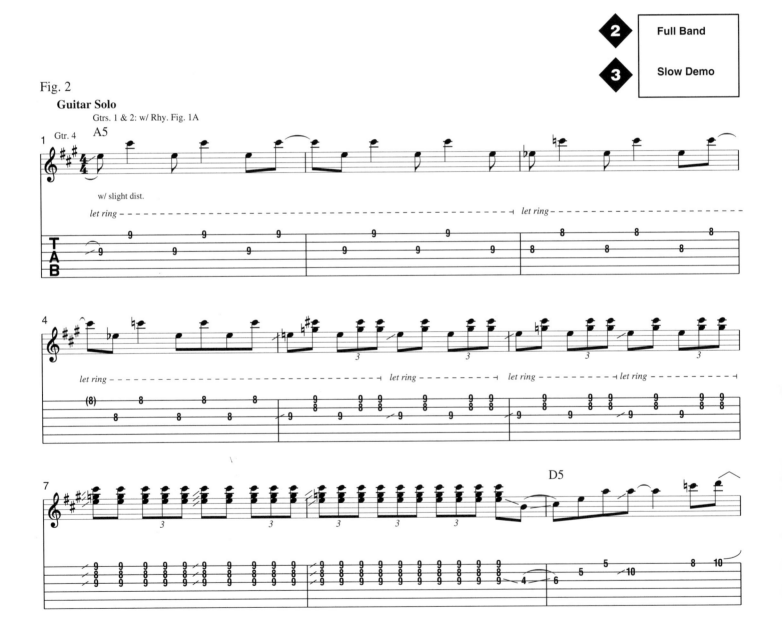

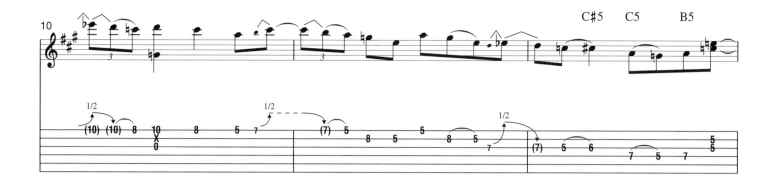

CAN'T YOU SEE

Words and Music by Toy Caldwell
Performed by the Marshall Tucker Band on *The Marshall Tucker Band* in 1973

One of the many fine attributes of Southern Rock was the willingness of the various bands to experiment with instrumentation beyond the requisite keening guitars. Hailing from South Carolina, the Marshall Tucker Band often bolstered their sound with bleating horn sections and were especially daring by featuring a flute on "Can't You See" from their debut album. The blending of acoustic (horns, piano, and guitar) and electric (guitar, bass, and keyboards) instruments gave the Tuckers a foothold on the laid-back airwaves of the early seventies.

Despite the full complement of tonalities, the band was unquestionably a showcase for lead guitarist Toy Caldwell. In a genre boasting a truckload of talented Les Paul pickers, Caldwell stood out by virtue of his jazzy melodic sense expressed in the same manner as Wes Montgomery: with his bare thumb. Blessed with *beaucoup* chops, he casually tossed off "pick" harmonics with his thumb and thumbnail while spinning fluid, melodic lines blending blues, jazz, and country styles.

Figure 3–Intro

Measures 1–8 are played fingerstyle on an acoustic guitar (Gtr. 1). Try a three-finger (thumb, index, and middle) approach with the thumb accessing strings 6–4 and the index and middle fingers sharing strings 3–1. Either the thumb or index finger can be employed for the strummed chords. Gtr. 2 (acoustic) enters with the band at measure 9 and should be strummed with a pick. Observe that Rhy. Fig. 1 (measures 13–20 in slash notation) as played by Gtr. 2 also appears as the accompaniment to the chorus.

Toy Caldwell sounds similar to an alto saxophone as he ladles in his sweet-sounding Les Paul (following the bucolic flute) beginning in measure 13. His choice runs are derived almost entirely from the root position of the B (relative minor) blues scale. Inasmuch as the chords are fairly basic and firmly rooted in D Mixolydian tonality, Caldwell plays more by "feel" than with any sort of conscious effort to "follow the changes."

Consequently, there is a good deal of emphasis on the root note (D) with the occasional tasty bend of the 2nd (E) up to the melodic major 3rd (F♯). In other words, soloing over this type of progression mainly requires creating tension by playing notes "away" from the root and then resolving to it. One significant exception to this concept occurs in measures 19 and 20. Here Caldwell moves to the root position of the G major scale (third position) and the D major scale (second position), respectively.

4 | Full Band

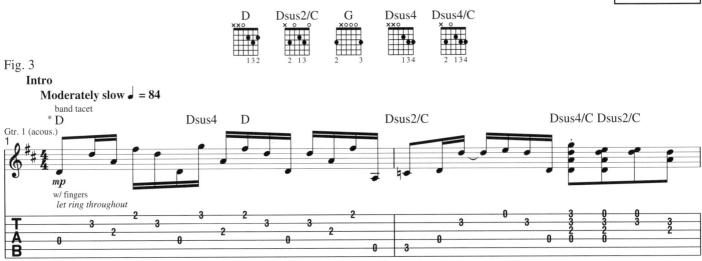

Fig. 3

Intro

Moderately slow ♩ = 84

* Chord symbols reflect overall harmony.

** Strum w/ R.H. finger.

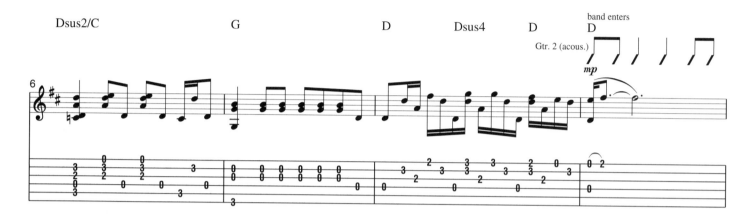

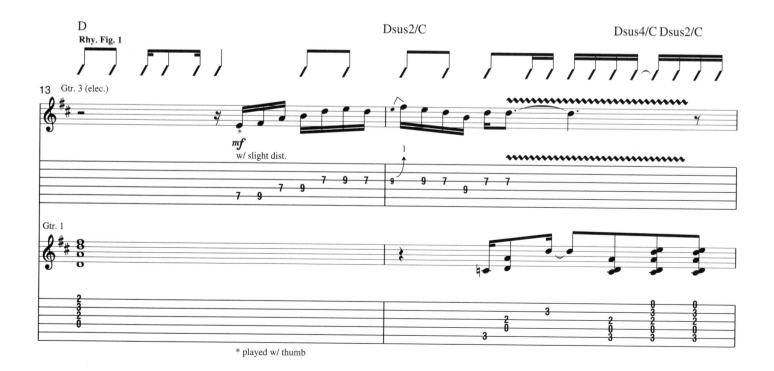

* played w/ thumb

Figure 4–Guitar Solo 3

Guitar Solo 3 begins with a tasty bend from E to F♯. Continuing with the same scale choices as in the verses and choruses, Toy slinks about in the root position of the B blues scale in measures 1–4, emphasizing the melodic major 3rd (F♯) and the root (D) notes. Starting on the "and" of beat 4 in measure 4 (I), however, Caldwell begins executing a time-warping, double-string bend that continues through measure 5 (I). Moving out of the B blues scale into the root position of the D blues scale, he pushes the B (6th) note at fret 12 one-half step to C (♭7th) while simultaneously raising the G (4th) a full step to A (5th). Dig that pulling *down* on both strings with the index or ring finger naturally jacks up the pitch of the two strings an unequal amount due to the physics of the guitar fingerboard. The resulting dominant harmony over the sus4 chords creates a nice bluesy tension, which is resolved to the stable and consonant 5th (A) in measure 6.

In measure 7 (IV), Caldwell returns to the root position of the B blues scale where the notes A, B, D, E, and F♯ function as the hip 9th, 3rd, 5th, 6th, and *major 7th* over the G major harmony. Staying in position, he wraps up by resolving to the root note (D) over the I chord in measure 8.

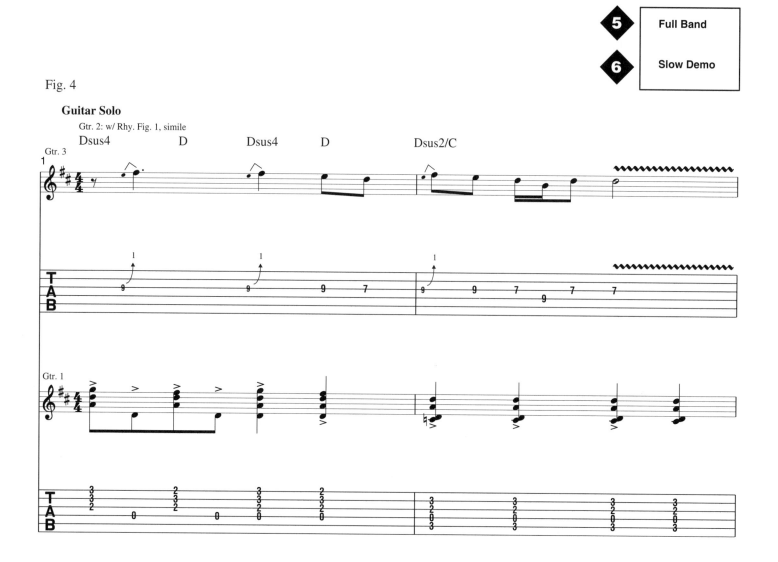

Fig. 4

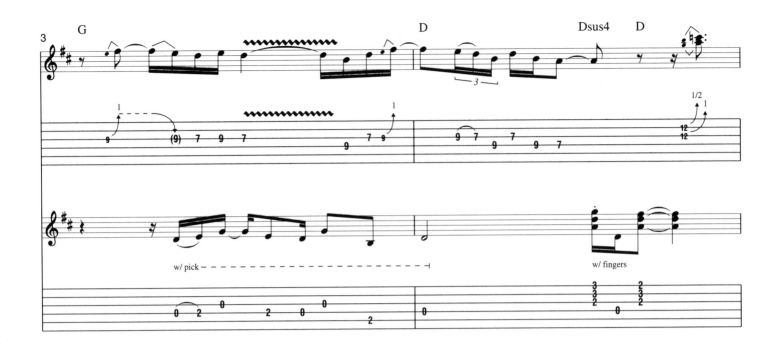

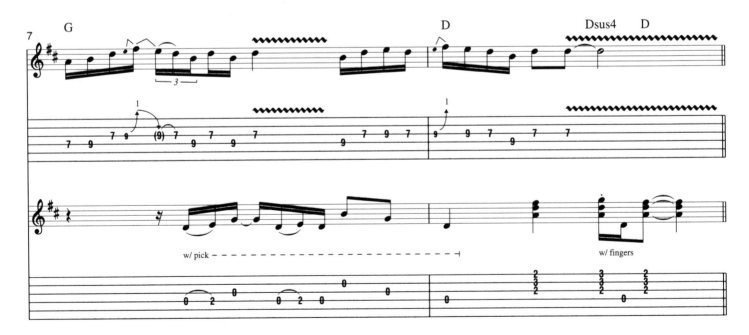

CAUGHT UP IN YOU

Words and Music by Frank Sullivan, Jim Peterik, Jeff Carlisi and Don Barnes
Performed by 38 Special on *Special Forces* in 1982

38 Special could be considered second generation Southern rockers, even though they staked out their turf in 1975—only a few years after Lynyrd Skynyrd, the Marshall Tucker Band, and other "wild-eyed Southern boys." From the mid-seventies on, fads and fashions changed rapidly, a situation greatly exacerbated by the birth of MTV in 1981. Led by lead singer Donnie Van Zant (brother of Ronnie *and* Johnnie), 38 Special managed to maintain a productive career into the nineties by graduating from good-time, "let me hear ya' say yeah!" boogie to tuneful arena rock in the early eighties.

"Caught Up in You," cowritten by Jim Peterik and Frank Sullivan (keyboardist and guitarist, respectively, for Survivor), soared to #11 in July 1982. More hit singles followed with "Second Chance" making it all the way to #10 in 1989. The next album, *Rock & Roll Strategy*, would be the swan song for this underrated band. Between 1991 and 1997, no recordings were released. In 1999, *Live at Sturgis* followed *Resolution* as a comeback attempt.

Figure 5–Verse

The verse is composed of four four-measure phrases. Gtrs. 1 and 2 divide the fingerboard into the lower and upper registers by string choice and indicate the chord changes with double stops in 3rds, 4ths, and 5ths. In a stroke of rhythmic brilliance, the chords have been arranged to change on the "and" of beats 2 and 4, thereby adding with anticipation to the propulsive nature of the staccato, palm-muted, eighth-note strums. Be sure to notice the way the chords are perceived to dramatically descend in recurring cycles until the last three measures, where they climactically ascend A–A#°–B.

* Chord symbols represent overall harmony.

when I'd be say-in' to you, "Don't let this good ___ love slip ___ a - way, ___

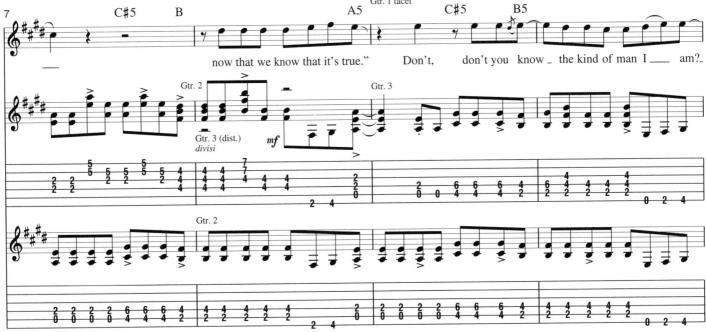

now that we know that it's true." Don't, don't you know ___ the kind of man I ___ am? ___

___ No, said I'd nev - er fall in love a - gain. ___ But it's real and the feel -

* composite arrangement

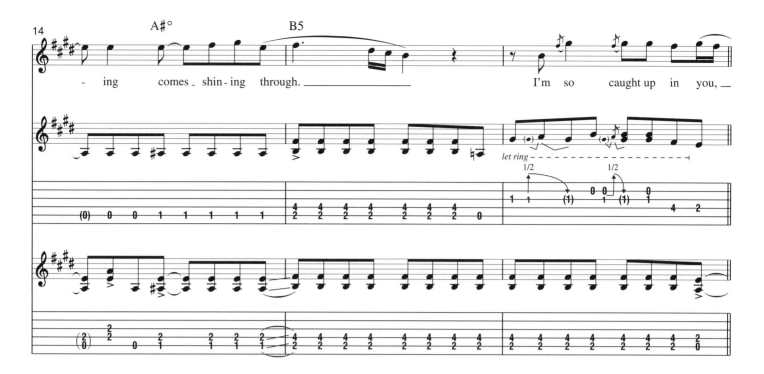

Figure 6–Second Chorus

The chords descend and ascend similarly in the chorus with Gtrs. 2 & 3 (Rhy. Figs. 1 and 1A) maintaining the rhythmic pulse. Gtr. 4 is layered in, however, with a complementary arpeggiated figure. Check out how the high E string drones over each chord voicing, providing a *common tone* throughout the progression.

Beginning in measure 2, Gtr. 5 (Carlisi) tosses off a long ascending run derived from the C♯ minor pentatonic scale (with the addition of the A) that is a virtual lesson in how to connect all five positions in the scale over the course of an octave. Based mostly on "feel" rather than "playing the changes," Carlisi finishes with a super-cool chromatic passage in measures 11–14 of G♯–A–A♯–B that intensifies the matching ascending chords.

8 **Full Band**

Fig. 6

Second Chorus

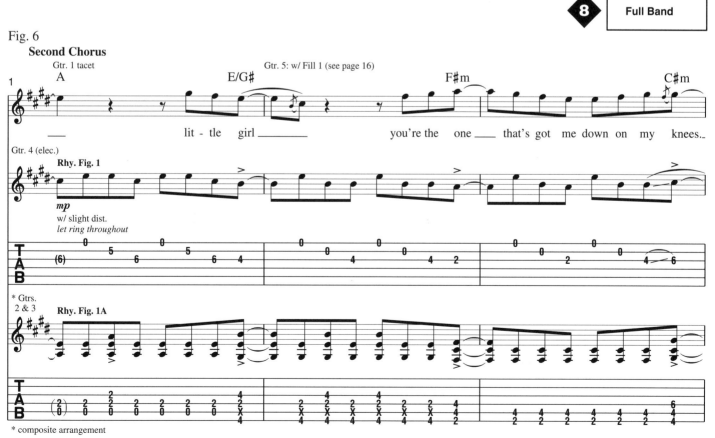

* composite arrangement

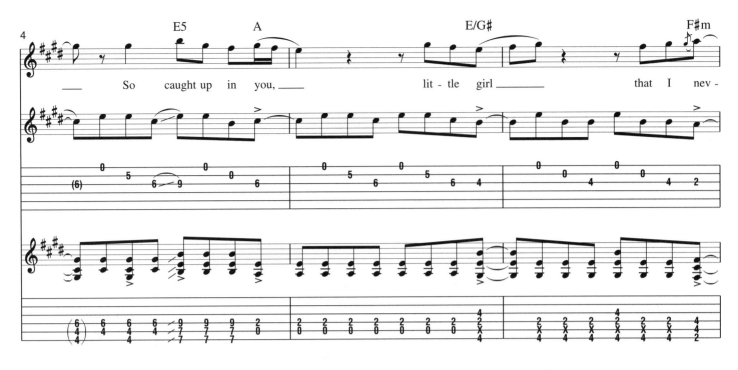

So caught up in you, _____ lit-tle girl _____ that I nev-

-er wan-na get my-self free. _____ And ba-by, it's true. _____ You're the one _____ who caught

Fill 1
Gtr. 5 (dist.)

mp

mf

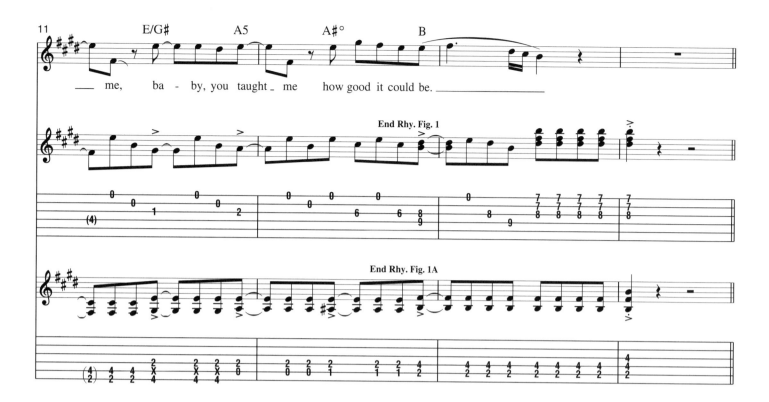

Figure 7–Guitar Solo

Carlisi (Gtr. 5) evolves the C♯ minor pentatonic scale into the C♯ Aeolian mode for even more melodic note choices as he sails his Les Paul over the chord changes. More importantly, in a solo that sounds spontaneous, he makes several deliberate decisions about note selection. Right off the bat, he sustains and vibratos the root (A) over the A5 in measure 1. In measure 2, he does the same with E (root of E/G♯), while on the "and" of beat 4 in measure 3 and beats 1 and 2 of measure 4 (C♯m), he wiggles the root (C♯). In measures 6 and 7, he follows the E/G♯, F♯m, and C♯m with the root notes as well.

Carlisi steps "outside the box" in measures 9 and 10 by injecting a series of cool octaves played on strings 1 and 3. Using the E major scale as a springboard, he shimmys up the neck C♯–D♯–E–F♯–G♯ over A, E/G♯, and F♯5, segueing smoothly into the E major scale in measure 11. In measures 12–13, he nails the "and" of beat 4 with a whole-step bend that targets a strong chord tone of the B harmony—the root note. This climactic phrase is heightened by the addition of an overdubbed harmony guitar in 3rds and 4ths (á la Duane and Dickey).

9 Full Band

10 Slow Demo
Gtr. 5

Fig. 7

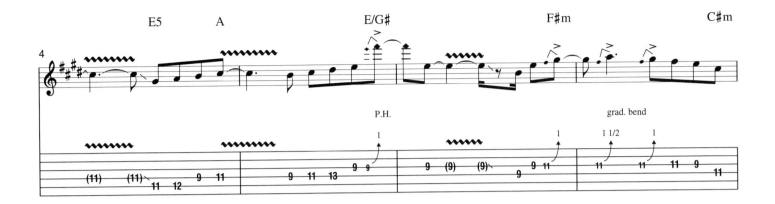

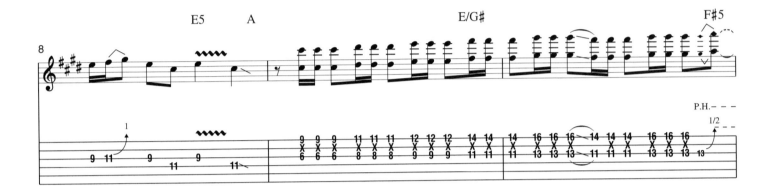

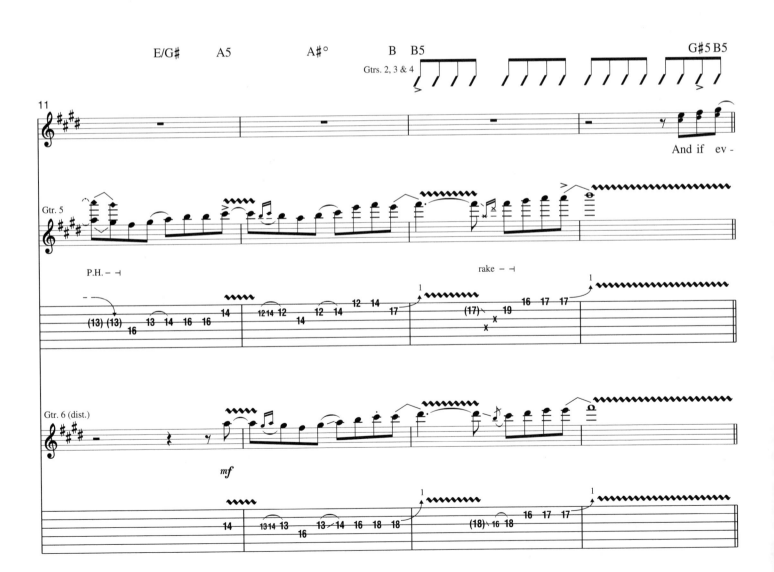

COMIN' HOME

Words and Music by Eric Clapton and Bonnie Bramlett
Performed by Delaney & Bonnie & Friends as a single in 1970

Probably the biggest turning point in Eric "Slowhand" Clapton's vaunted career was joining Delaney and Bonnie Bramlett's traveling caravan in 1970 and recording "Comin' Home." This rollicking troupe of American and English musicians in 1969–70 included, at one time or another, Duane Allman, George Harrison, Leon Russell, and Dave Mason. The material reflected Delaney Bramlett's eclectic, artistic vision based around Southern blues, folk, and country music he had been performing with his wife Bonnie since 1967.

Though Clapton wrote the music and Bonnie wrote the lyrics, Delaney's lead vocal would seem to have had more than a little influence on the immediate singing style of E.C. Equally important, the overdubbed, orchestrated guitars would be heard on "Let It Rain" from *Eric Clapton* and most spectacularly on "Layla." Not to be overlooked, Clapton's choice of a Strat (as opposed to the ES-335 he had played with Blind Faith and various other Kalamazoo instruments with Cream) signaled a sea of change in the rock world from fat-bottom Gibsons to crackling Fenders.

Figure 8–Verse

The verses are monochord (A) grooves with Delaney engaging in "call and response" with Gtrs. 1 and 3. With Gtr. 2 vamping around the open A position with broken chords (A) and blues scale licks, Gtr. 3 plays a repeating two-measure melodic lick in the root position of the A basic blues scale with the prominent addition of the major 3rd (C#). Gtr. 1 plays the harmony in 3rds, 5ths, and 6ths at the twelfth position.

Figure 9–Guitar Solo

Gtr. 2 vamps on an E5 (V) chord, while Gtr. 1 takes an eight-measure ride in the E basic blues scale. With no harmonic movement, Clapton just wrings the hell out of the ♭3rd (G), 4th (A), 5th (B), and root (E) notes. Check out the tension-producing, Chuck Berry-style (via T-Bone Walker) unison bend with 5ths that E.C. inserts for a jaunty rock 'n' roll touch.

12 Full Band

13 Slow Demo
Gtr. 1

Fig. 9

21

DIXIE ROCK

Words and Music by Maurice Hirsch, James Hall and Jack Hall
Performed by Wet Willie on _Dixie Rock_ in 1975

It is likely that, even today, after all the salacious reportage oozing out of the Clinton White House during the nineties, many people do not get the double-entendre of "Wet Willie." Be that as it may, the Willies were one of the more original bands to come bopping out of Alabama. Their influences were much closer to R&B and Memphis soul (with gospel touches as purveyed by Stax/Volt Records) than the heavy British blues-rock infusing the Allman Brothers, Lynyrd Skynyrd, and the other jam bands that followed.

Begun in the late sixties by brothers Jimmy (vocals, sax) and Jack Hall (bass) with guitarist Ricky Hirsch, their move to Macon, Georgia in 1970 gave them access to Capricorn Records. Signing with the label that claimed both the ABB and the Marshall Tucker Band, Willie had a good run until 1978. Basing their sound around Jimmy Hall's blue-eyed soul shout and strong, groove-oriented songs, they were still capable of stretching out instrumentally and letting Hirsch wail.

In 1978, Wet Willie switched labels to Epic with only Jimmy Hall and keyboardist Michael Duke held over from the previous incarnation. In 1980, they finally threw in the towel. Hirsch went on as a sideman into the mid-nineties with Joan Armatrading, the Allman Brothers, Lenny McDaniel, and Billy Vera. Though "Keep on Smilin'" from the self-titled LP in 1974 was a bigger hit, "Dixie Rock" has maintained its niche as an FM classic and a banner for "Dixie rockers" everywhere.

Figure 10–Verse

The verse is eight measures of basically a one-measure vamp consisting of D5 (I), Csus2 (♭VII), and G/B (IV). On paper it bears a superficial relationship to Skynyrd's "Sweet Home Alabama," but Gtrs. 1 and 2 (composite arrangement) let open, broken chords sustain for a droning effect. Performance tip: Start with your left hand in an open D major formation.

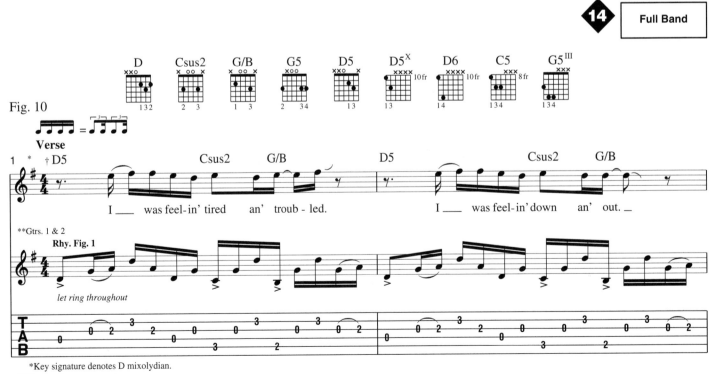

*Key signature denotes D mixolydian.
**Composite arrangement
†Chord symbols reflect overall tonality.

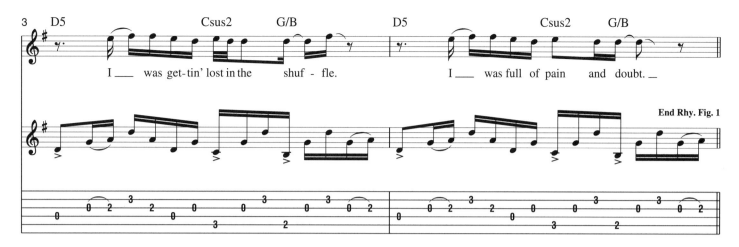

Figure 11–Chorus

One of the distinctive characteristics of "Dixie Rock" is the double-time feel in the chorus, bridge, and guitar solo. Put simply, the drummer accents every beat of the 4/4 time signature, rather than just beats 2 and 4 (backbeats), making the particular passage feel like the measures are going by twice as fast. The resulting dynamics really kick the tune in the butt.

Gtrs. 3 and 4 combine for a horn-like harmony lick in the four-measure chorus that functions as a hook and can easily be executed on one guitar. With your index finger on the G♯ and your middle finger on the F (E♯), bend both notes up one half step in measures 1 and 3. In measures 2 and 4, sustain and vibrato F and D with your middle and ring fingers.

As accompaniment, Gtr. 1 chunks away on open-position chords as shown, while Gtr. 2 rocks hard with driving boogie patterns. If performing "Dixie Rock" with two guitarists (or guitar and keyboards), one should play the harmony lick, while the other plays the boo-gie pattern.

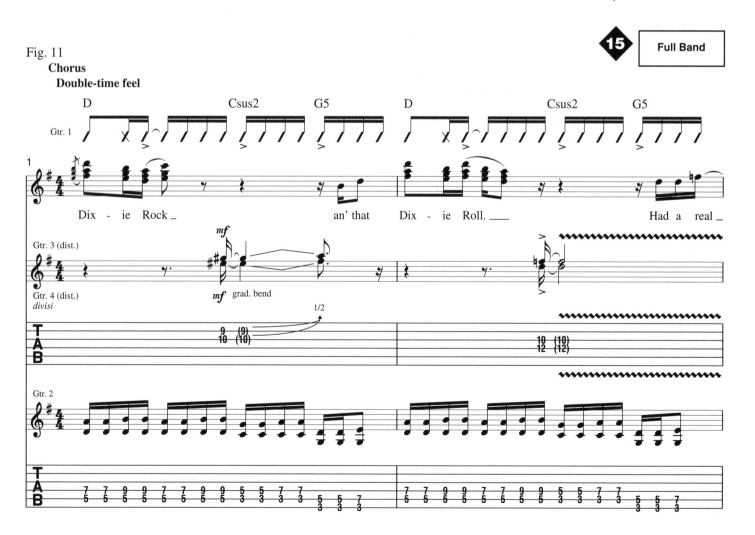

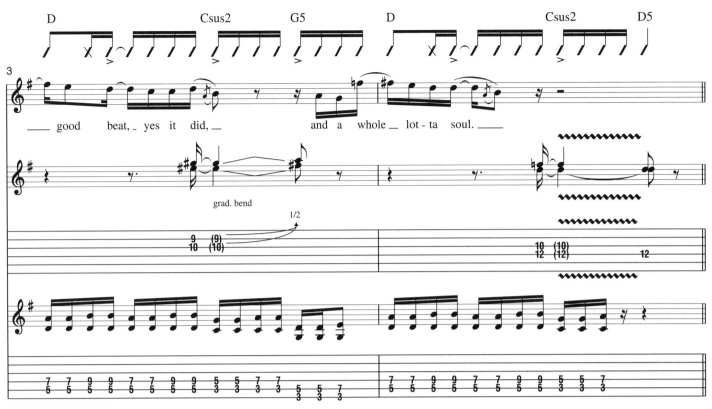

Figure 12–Guitar Solo

Over a V–IV–I chord sequence featuring 5ths and 6ths on the V, Ricky Hirsch parleys the E minor scale (a fave of Southern rockers!) into a melodic and rhythmically snappy musical statement. Like a true craftsman, he builds a handsome edifice step by step. Most impressive is how tangy, half-step bends of the 3rd (B) to the 4th (C) lead to a rapid-fire series of three repeating and escalating patterns. In measure 3, he plays E (6th), D (5th), B (3rd), D, and B on the bass strings. In measure 4, he moves up to A (2nd), F♯ (major 7th!), E, F♯, A, and F♯. Finally, in measure 5, Hirsch shifts up the neck to A, B, A, and F♯. In the remaining six measures (the progression changes to match the verse chords), he flies up to the extension position of the E minor scale between frets 15 and 17, with soaring lyrical bends and humming vibrato.

16 **Full Band**

17 **Slow Demo**
Gtr. 4

Fig. 12

Guitar Solo
Double-time feel

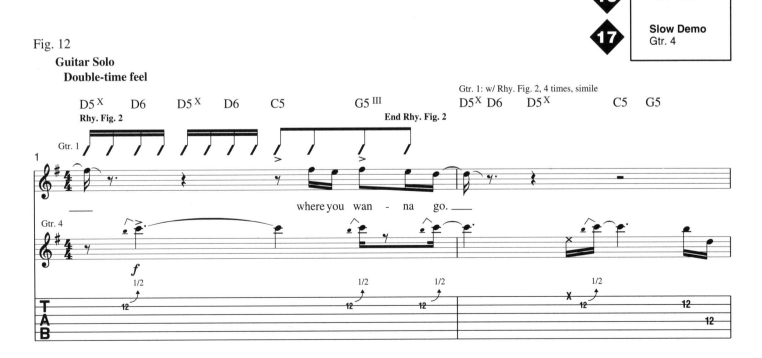

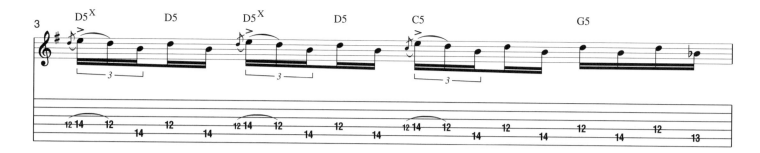

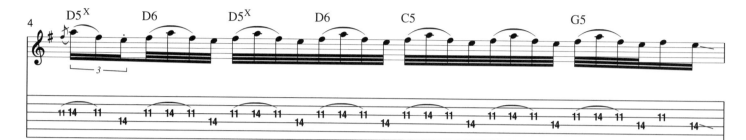

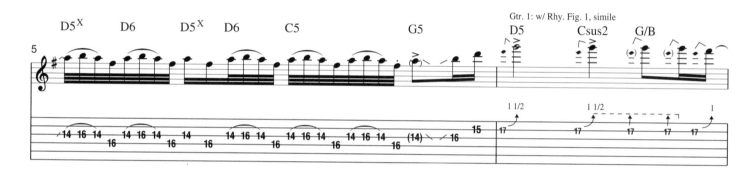

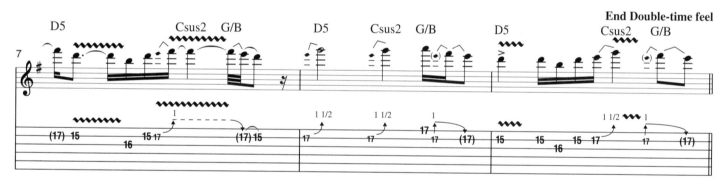

FLIRTIN' WITH DISASTER

Words and Music by Danny Joe Brown, David L. Hlubek and Banner H. Thomas
Performed by Molly Hatchet on *Flirtin' With Disaster* in 1979

With guitarists Dave Hlubek, Steve Holland, and Duane Roland wielding their axes like weapons, Molly Hatchet cut a wide swath up the FM dial in the late seventies. Three years after getting together in 1975, the Jacksonville, Florida band recorded their self-titled debut album, which soon went platinum. *Flirtin' with Disaster* followed in 1979 with even bigger success, selling over two million copies. It looked like the wild boys named for a notorious Southern prostitute alleged to have sliced and diced her "johns" were on their way to mega-success. In 1980, however, personnel and musical changes diverted the Hatchet men from their guitar boogie mission, and their popularity began trailing off. In 1985, the group took a hiatus, only to return in 1989 without first lead guitarist Hlubek. In 1996, they reunited and released *Lightning Strikes Twice,* followed in 1998 by *Silent Reign of Heroes.*

"Flirtin' with Disaster" is a rockin' boogie butt-kicker somewhat reminiscent of Lynyrd Skynyrd numbers like "Call Me the Breeze." Like L.S., the "Hatchets" favored fat, bottom-heavy, British-type crunchy distortion as their fuel of choice.

Figure 13–Verse 1

The sixteen-measure verse consists of four four-measure phrases of A–A–G–A voiced in pumping 5ths and 6ths played by Gtrs. 2 and 3 in unison.

Performance Tip: Two guitars, with one taking the part of Gtrs. 2 and 3, could easily play the verse.

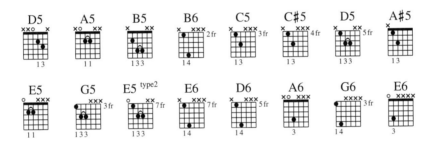

Figure 14–Chorus

The chorus is divided into two sections. The first, sixteen measures in length, is built upon four four-measure phrases of B5–B–E, E–B, D–A, and B voiced as triads and triple stops with accompanying embellishments. The second section, twenty-four measures long, levitates the tune by advancing a hip minor 3rd to D and features Gtr. 1 punctuating the B change (measures 3–4 and 11–12) with punchy root-position B minor pentatonic licks.

Fig. 14

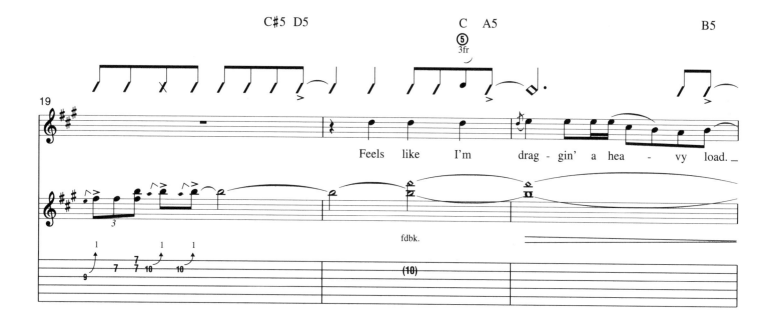

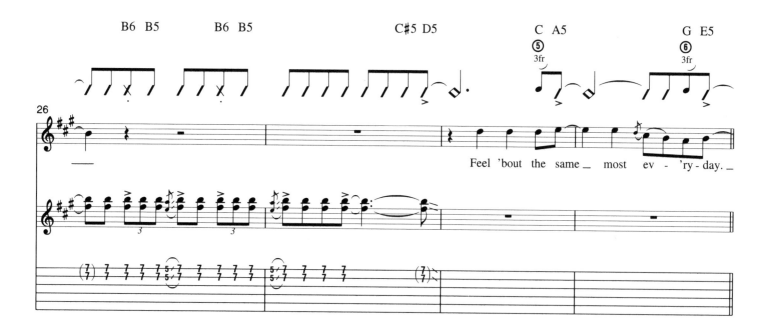

Figure 15–Interlude and Guitar Solo

After verse 2 and chorus 2, the sixteen-measure second ending drops into a half-time feel. In contrast, however, Gtr. 1 plays melodic fills based on the major scale of each chord change while Gtrs. 2 and 3 sustain power chords over each change. In measures 1–32 of the forty-eight-measure solo, Gtr. 1 flashes its way through four eight-measure progressions of E–E–D–D–A–G–E–E that *sound* like a key change to E from A. In fact, that is exactly the way it is played, with the E minor pentatonic scale employed in various positions. Dig the highlights: 1) A hypnotic climb from fret 12–15 in measures 15 and 16 that peaks with a bend to the root (E) at fret 22) The classic ascending and descending triplet run in measures 17–24. 3) A melodious ascending run up the C♯ minor scale in measures 25–27 that, along with the next five measures of the C♯ minor scale, provides a smooth transition to the climactic measures that follow.

In measures 33–40, Gtrs. 4 and 5 blend their voices with Gtr. 1 to create a three-part celestial harmony. Notice that the top voice of the melody is drawn again from the C♯ minor scale. It's hard to believe that such a glorious instrumental climax began innocently enough back in the intro with the eighth-note bass line!

30

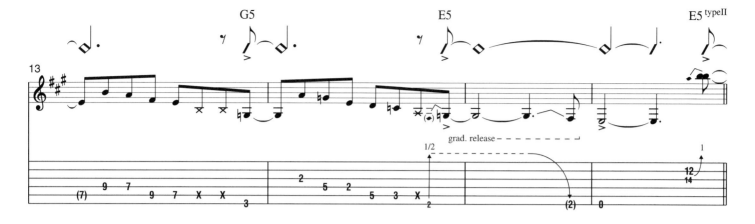

Guitar Solo

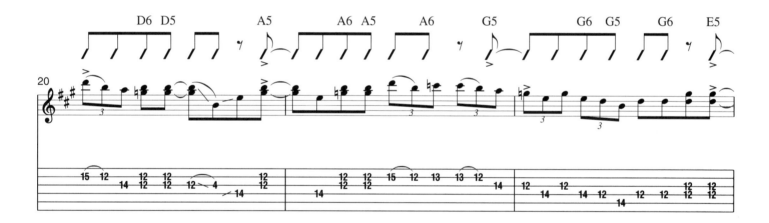

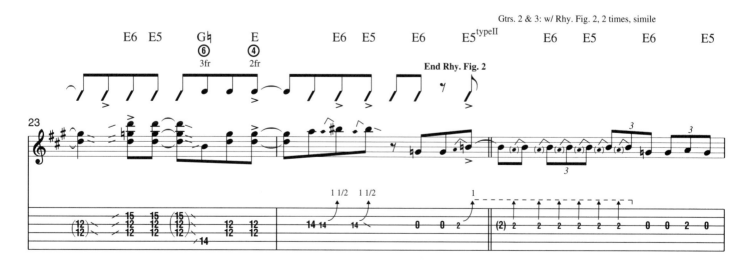

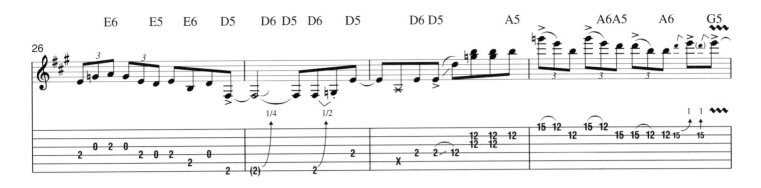

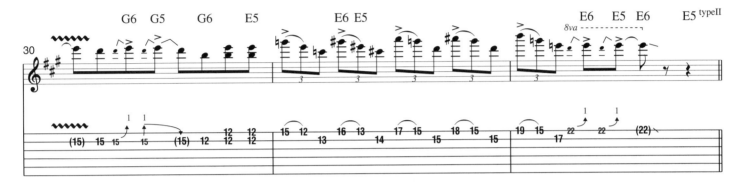

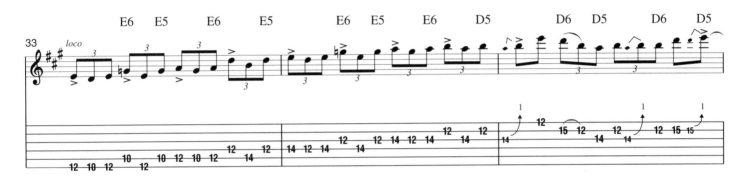

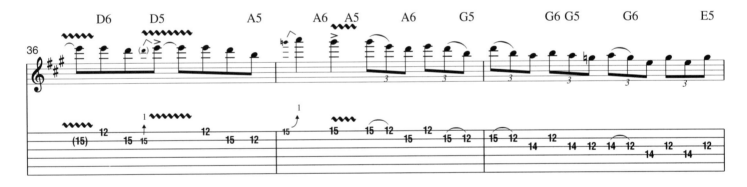

GREEN GRASS AND HIGH TIDES

Words and Music by Hughie Thomasson Jr.
Performed by the Outlaws on *Outlaws* in 1975

In the annals of triple-guitar extravaganzas, two organic and orgasmic master-pieces stand out: Lynyrd Skynyrd's "Freebird," the blueprint for all others, and the Outlaws' "Green Grass and High Tides."

Guitarists and singers Hughie Thomasson and Henry Paul started the Outlaws in Tampa, Florida in 1972. They added Billy Jones as the third axeman a year later. In 1975, they released their self-titled debut featuring the Top 40 hit "There Goes Another Love Song" and the anthemic "Green Grass and High Tides." In a familiar story, wholesale per-sonnel changes began to take place in the late seventies. In 1979, *Ghost Riders in the Sky* produced another Top 40 single with the title track, but by 1982, only Thomasson remained from the original lineup, and the band split. Within a year, he and Paul had reformed the Outlaws, only to have Paul leave again in 1986 and reappear with Blackhawk in 1994. Meanwhile, Thomasson joined a revamped Lynyrd Skynyrd while still leading the Outlaws. Coincidentally, tragedy had struck the Outlaws as it did Skynyrd, when original guitarist Billy Jones and bassist Frank O'Keefe died within weeks of each other in 1985. In 2000, Thomasson and company released *So-Low*.

Figure 16–Intro

With the anthemic sequence of Em–C–G–D–A (vi–IV–I–V–II) as the core pro-gression, the Outlaws begin building a head of steam in the intro. Gtr. 1 arpeggiates with four eighth notes on each chord until the A, which is sustained in measure 3 and then given a dynamic rest in measure 4. Starting with the second ending, Gtrs. 2 and 3 dupli-cate the pattern in unison, adding sixteenth notes in measures 5 and 6 that hint at the acceleration to come. Beginning in measure 9, Gtrs. 2 and 3 accent the downbeat of each arpeggiated chord with full, strummed chords for a dramatic orchestral effect. Measures 13–20 kick it up to a double-time feel with briskly strummed broken chords played by all three guitarists. This gives way to Gtr. 1 ripping in the E minor pentatonic scale in mea-sures 17 and 18. (Performance tip: If you're the only guitarist, play Gtr. 1 throughout. With two guitars, play the parts of Gtrs. 1 and 2.)

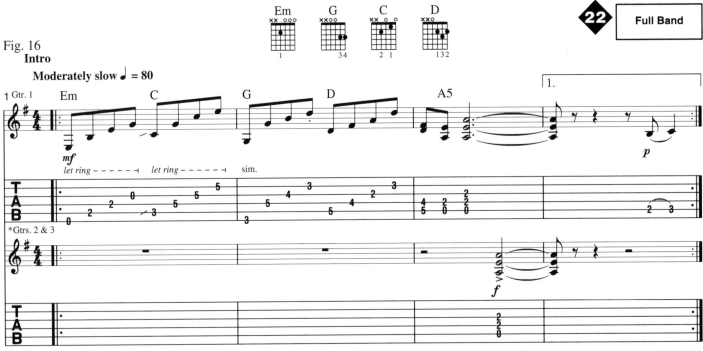

*composite arrangement

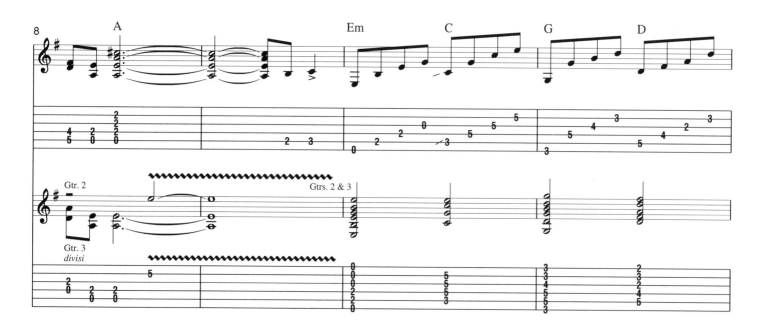

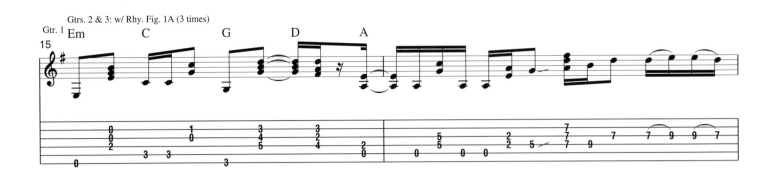

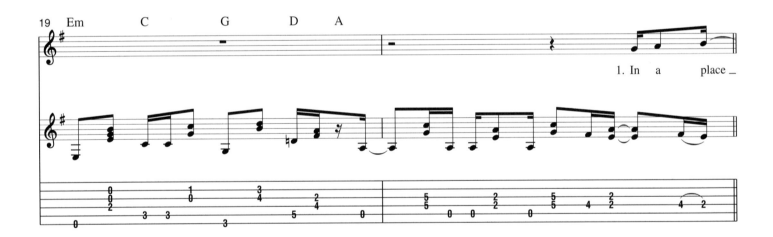

Figure 17–Verse 1

The band eases back from double time and settles into a syncopated, almost funky groove. The progression of Em–G–C–D is executed by Gtr. 1 and Gtr. 2 (Rhy. Fig. 2) with tasty chordal embellishment and bass runs reminiscent of Jimi Hendrix's voodoo magic on songs like "Little Wing" and "Castles Made of Sand," while Gtr. 3 chunks away on chords (Rhy. Fig. 3).

Performance Tip: With two guitars, play the parts of Gtrs. 1 and 2. In addition, use the index finger on the C and D triads (frets 5 and 7) to access the hammer-on and pull-off embellishments.

Fig. 17

Verse

End double-time feel

Figure 18–First 28 measures of Guitar Solo

With the verse chord progression as a gracefully undulating vehicle for improvisation, Gtr. 1 winds his way up the E minor pentatonic scale, while Gtrs. 2 and 3 play Rhy. Figs. 2 and 3, respectively. The open position emphasizes his spanky, twangy tone as he whips out line after line of punchy hammer-ons and pull-offs spiked with slinky bends from A to B and released down to G. As the chords go by too quickly to pick out target notes over the changes, the solo concept consists of wave after wave of tension and resolution to the root (E). Starting in measure 9, however, he relocates to the seventh position and works loosely from the Em barre chord form, creating ringing harmonies with double stops. Beginning in measure 16, he moves to the fifth position in order to access notes relative to both the C and D chords. Building even more layers of harmony, he heads back to the seventh position in measure 19 to add the G and E notes at frets 8 and 9, respectively, along with the barre at fret 7 for a rich chordal effect. He then leads to a logical and brilliant conclusion starting in measure 23, as he plays around at fret 7 over the Em and G chords. He follows this with a move to fret 5 for the C and D chords, alternating every other measure in this way until measure 28.

Fig. 18

Guitar Solo

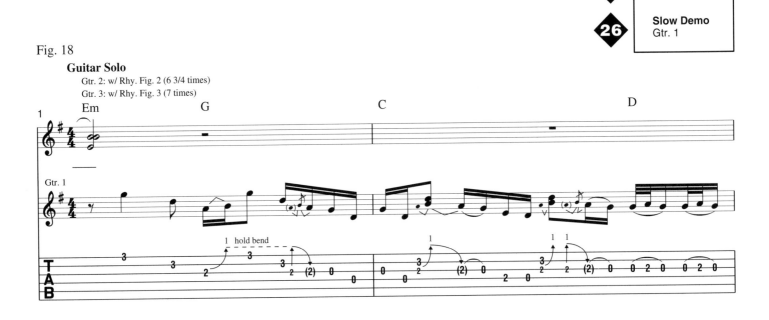

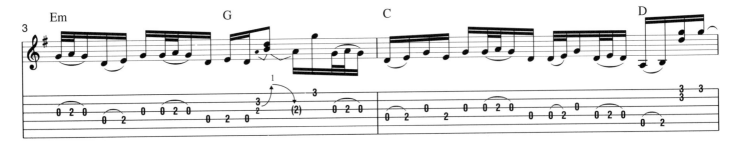

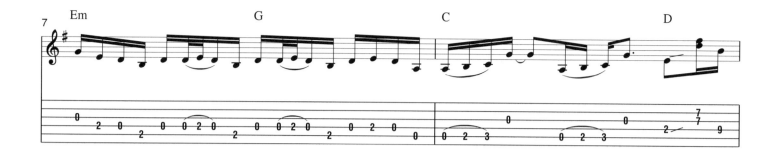

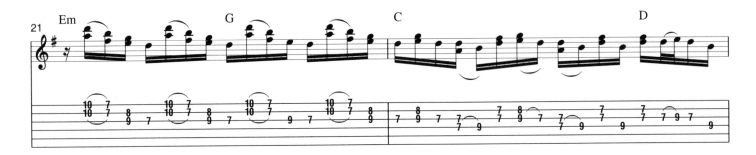

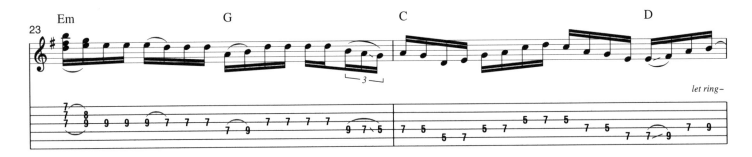

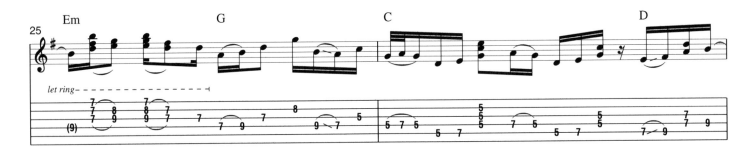

Figures 19, 20, 21, 22, 23, 24, 25–Outro Solos

In Fig. 19, the three Outlaws come out galloping in measures 1–4 with the double-time rhythm previewed in the intro. Gtr. 1 immediately settles into the box around the seventh position after swooping in with a moaning, one-and-a-half step bend (E to G) on string 3 (measures 5–12). As in the previous solo, he takes advantage of the proximity to the root note (E) at fret 9 and the double-stop harmonies available at fret 7 and fret 5. Repeating single-note patterns are part of the "signature licks" prevalent throughout the solo, and Gtr. 1 fires off a dandy in measure 10 (IV chord). Rapidly bending the A to A# (Bb), he releases the bend and pulls off to the G, resolving to the E.

In measure 1 (Fig. 20), Gtr. 1 pummels the low E string with a breathtaking run up the E minor pentatonic scale beginning with the open string and concluding in measure 2 with strings 2 and 1 open. Functioning as an aural signpost into the next section, Gtr. 1 performs an amazing bit of "sleight o' hand" with a wildly exuberant series of octaves (measures 3–8). Played entirely on strings 5 and 3 with emphasis on the E notes (frets 7 and 9), he jigs on up to frets 12 and 14 for the A notes played over the A chord in measure 8. Fig. 21 contains another smoking sextuplet in the octave root position of the E scale involving the D pulled off to B followed by the G, creating musical tension that is released in measure 4 as a transition to the next movement of this "symphony for three electric guitars."

Measures 1–4 (Fig. 22) function as a bridge between the solos of Gtr. 1 and Gtr. 2 over Em and A for two measures each. The double-time feel ceases, and both guitars play complementary parts involving a walk up the low E string from E to A in measures 1 and 3. This is alternated with an ascending scalar run for Gtr. 1 in measures 2 and 4. Beginning in measure 5, Gtr. 2 picks up the gauntlet and finds home at the ninth position. Making his own indelible statement on the tune with an explosive burst of energy, he bends the root (E) up one step to the cool 9th (F#) in measure 5, then vibratos the root note like a man possessed in measure 6. In measure 9, he steps outside of the E minor pentatonic scale to include F# from the E Aeolian mode for a subtle touch of melodic variation. Measures 10–12 (end of Fig. 22) contain a hip bend of the root to the 9th against the 4th (A) that engenders a nice bit of musical tension and anticipation. This resolves in measure 12, where the F# and A become the melodic 6th and root, respectively, of the IV (A) chord.

Gtr. 3 joins the fray at measure 1 (Fig. 23) and rattles off scorching repeating patterns in harmony with Gtr. 2 through measure 7. One of the technical, artistic, and emotional highpoints of "Green Grass and High Tides," it is thrilling to hear and even better to play! Close observation, by the way, reveals that the two guitarists are absolutely in sync rhythmically with their sextuplets, quintuplets, and quadruplets. In measure 1 (Fig. 24), Gtrs. 1 and 2 pull out a classic British quintuplet (think Jimmy Page in "Communication Breakdown") in the octave root position. Though an "oldie but a goodie," the surging nature of this lick is unbeatable for kicking forward momentum into overdrive.

At measure 1 (Fig. 25), Gtr. 2 repeats the sextuplet from measure 1 (Fig. 21), while Gtr. 1 plays the complementary harmony for a big finish.

Fig. 19

Outro-Solo
Double-time feel

Gtr. 1: w/ Rhy. Fig. 1 (2 times)
Gtrs. 2 & 3: w/ Rhy. Fig. 1A (6 times)

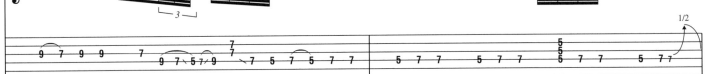

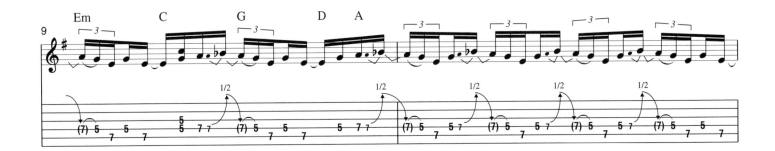

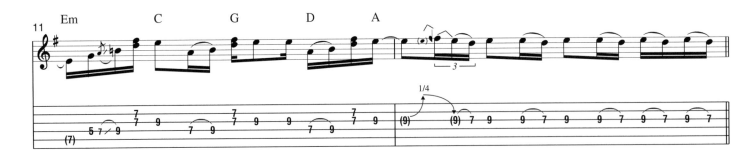

Fig. 20

Gtrs. 2 & 3: w/ Rhy. Fig. 1A (4 times)

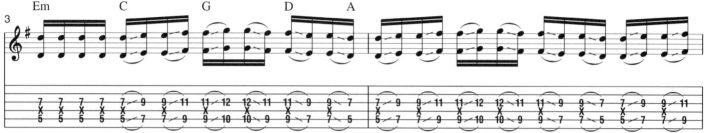

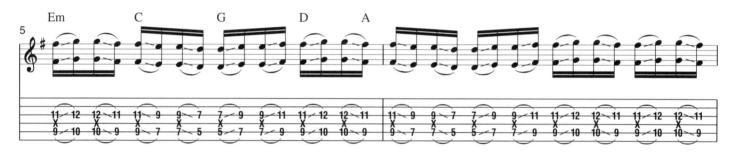

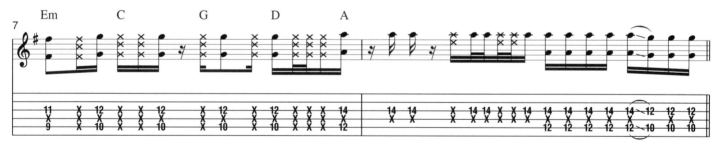

Fig. 21

Gtr. 2: w/ Rhy. Fig. 1A (2 times)

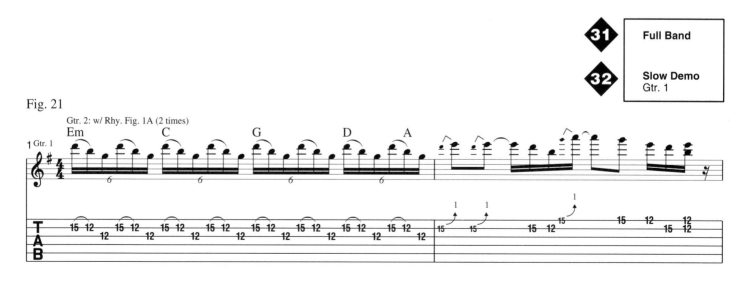

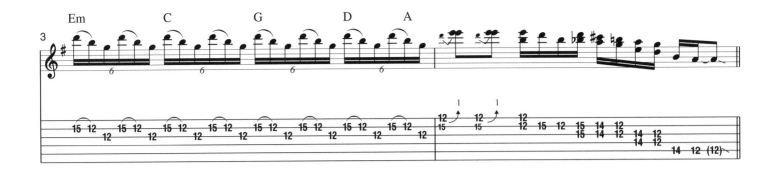

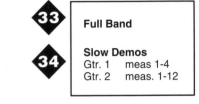

33 Full Band

34 Slow Demos
Gtr. 1 meas 1-4
Gtr. 2 meas. 1-12

Fig. 22

End double-time feel

Double-time feel

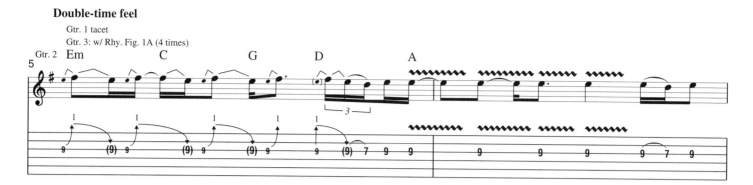

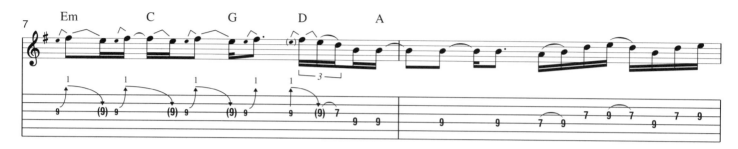

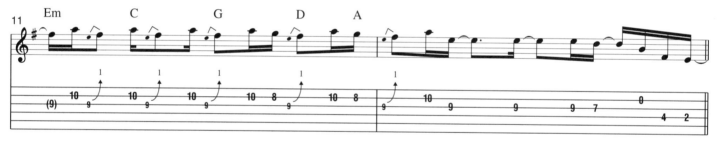

Fig. 23

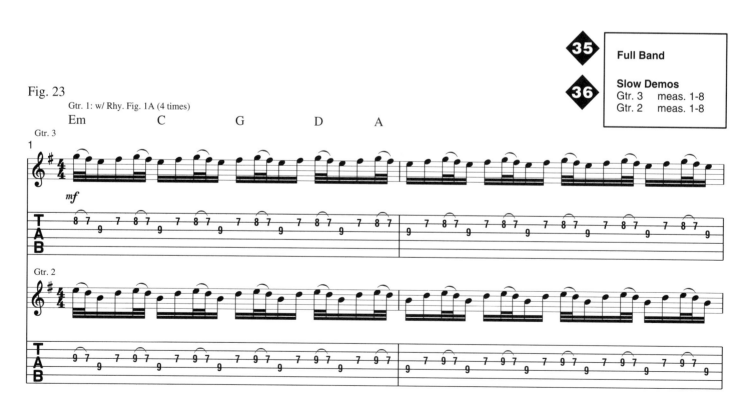

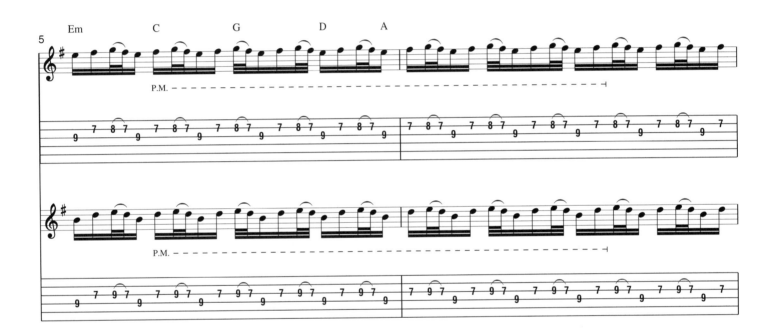

37 Full Band

38 Slow Demo

Fig. 24

*Gtrs. 1 & 2

*composite arrangement

39 Full Band

40 Slow Demo
Gtrs. 1 & 2

Fig. 25

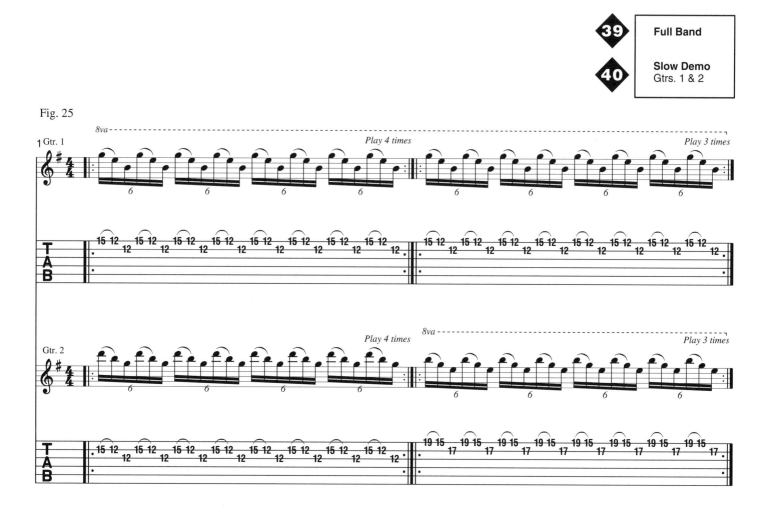

JIM DANDY

Words and Music by Lincoln Chase
Performed by Black Oak Arkansas on _High on the Hog_ in 1973

Every parent's nightmare in the libidinous seventies, Black Oak Arkansas reduced rock to the roll and shamelessly hawked sex to their audience. Named for their hometown in Arkansas, they were led by randy singer "Jim Dandy" Mangrum. Though sporting the classic Southern rock lineup with three guitarists in Ricky "Ricochet" Reynolds, Harvey "Burley" Jett, and Stan "Goober" Knight, Black Oak Arkansas were not virtuosos; they simply got by on sheer energy and raw boogie power.

The band started taking root in the mid-sixties, calling themselves Knowbody Else after they moved to New Orleans in 1969. They signed a contract with Stax Records in Memphis and produced a self-titled LP, released to no interest. They moved to MCA Records after changing their name to Black Oak Arkansas. Beginning with another self-titled record in 1971, they had a good ride into the mid-seventies. At this time, various personnel were upgraded, but the act and music were becoming stale. _Race with the Devil_ in 1977 and the modest hit "Strong Enough to Be Gentle" preceded a slide that brought the band to a standstill in 1980. Mangrum suffered a heart attack thereafter, but recorded solo albums in 1984 and 1986. In 1999, Black Oak Arkansas reformed and cut _The Wild Bunch_.

"Jim Dandy to the Rescue," featuring female singer Ruby Starr dueling and duetting with Mangrum, cracked the Top 30. Though its vocal crudeness bears little relation to Lavern Baker's slyly insinuating good humor (you can almost see Mangrum leering and rolling his eyes), the thumping shuffle and pithy solos give it a place in rock history.

Figure 26–Intro

The four-measure intro contains the two-measure rhythmic increment (shown in Rhy. Fig. 1) that underpins the entire arrangement. Notice the half-step slide from below the tonic (C7) that sets off each phrase (Gtr. 1).

Performance Tip: Use alternate pick strokes, taking into account that the eighth-note rests _would_ all be downstrokes if played.

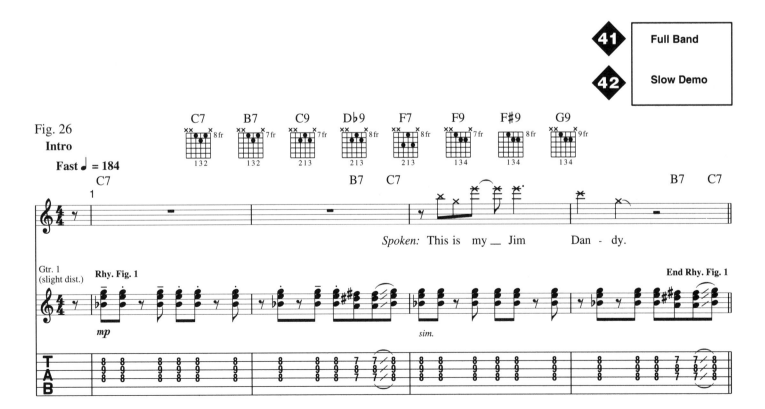

Figure 27–Chorus

Gtr. 1 vamps for eight measures on Rhy. Fig. 1, while Gtrs. 2 and 3 play a unison line that mimics the vocal. Observe that Gtr. 2 plays the C major-scale lick with slide in standard tuning.

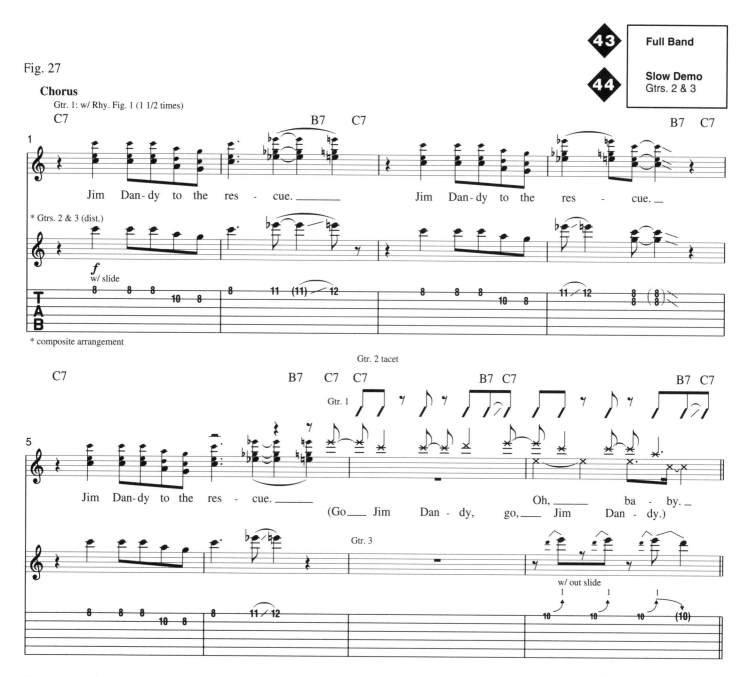

Fig. 27

Figure 28–Guitar Solo

Gtr. 3 kicks off this good-natured romp by cranking in the root and extension positions of the A minor pentatonic scale. Notice that the progression over which he solos is sixteen measures long. Measures 1–8 mirror those changes found in a 12-bar blues, but measures 9–16 are as follows: two measures of G (V), two measures of F (IV), and repeat. Following the changes in measures 1–8 like a good blues guitarist imitating a honking saxophone player from the fifties, Gtr. 3 emphasizes the root (C) and melodic 6th (A) over the I chord (C), and the 5th (C) and 3rd (A) over the IV chord (F). In measures 9–16, notes C, D, A, and E (bent up one step from the D) function as the sus4, 5th, 6th and major 3rd of the V (G) chord. Likewise, the C and A notes act as the 5th and major 3rd of the IV chord (F) as in measures 5 and 6.

Like a stealthy intruder, Gtr. 2 sneaks into measures 9–16 with a clever selection of repeating notes that support the V–IV changes. Over the V, he picks F (♭7th) and the hip E♭ (#5th) with the F bent up one step to the root (G). Over the IV, the F and E♭ function as the root and ♭7th. Also, check out the use of the C (5th) and B♭ (suspended 4th) notes, along with the E♭, in measures 12 and 15 of the IV chord.

In measure 16, Gtr. 2 begins a classic rock 'n' roll unison bend in 5ths (Chuck Berry courtesy of T-Bone Walker) and repeats it until measure 19, as Gtr. 3 hands off the solo like a relay race runner in measure 17. Desiring to create a big finish, Gtr. 2 shifts to a snappy triplet of E♭–C–G in measure 21 and repeats it until the end of the solo. The stop-time in measures 23 and 24 provide an additional dynamic effect.

Fig. 28

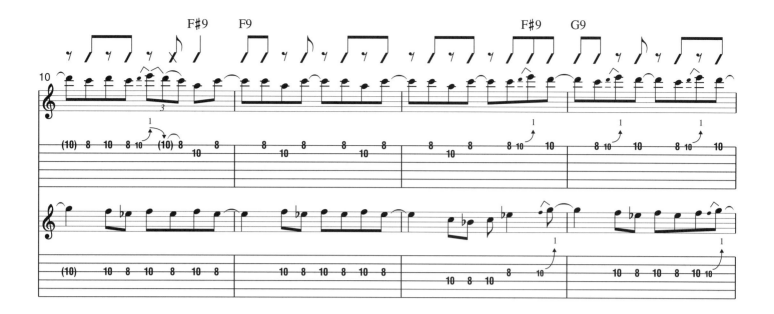

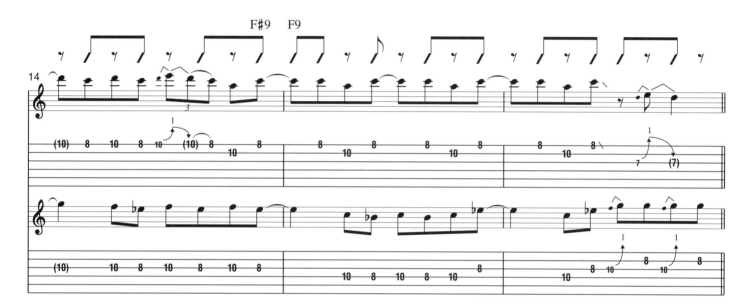

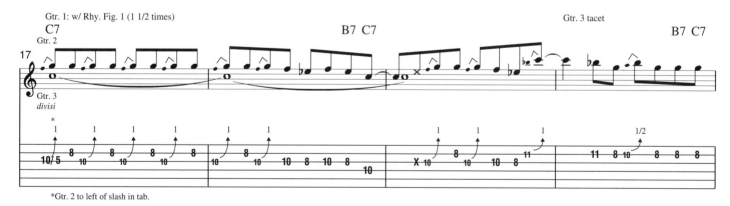

*Gtr. 2 to left of slash in tab.

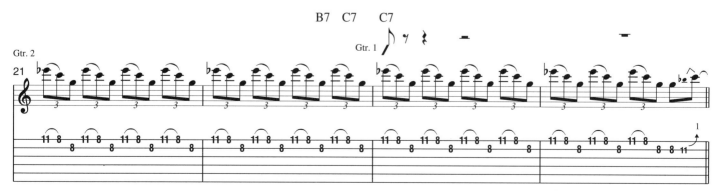

MELISSA

Words and Music by Gregg Allman and Steve Alaimo
Performed by the Allman Brothers Band on *Eat a Peach* in 1972

As the elder statesmen of Southern rock and one of America's greatest bands, The Allman Brothers Band have weathered more hard times than most in their thirty-year (and counting) career. In the process, they have managed to create an unmatched body of blues, country, and jazz-influenced rock.

Brothers Duane and Gregg Allman started the band in 1969 in Macon, Georgia. With two drummers, second guitarist Forrest Richard "Dickey" Betts adding twin harmony leads, and Gregg's Hammond B-3 and growling vocals, they produced a huge, grooving, pulsating sound. In concert, their jams were epic.

Starting with their self-titled debut in 1969 and continuing through *Idlewild South* (1970), *Live at Fillmore East* (1971), and *Eat a Peach* (1972), Duane's lead and slide guitar led ABB to heights of remarkable and ecstatic creativity. In October 1971, however, just after the release of *Live at Fillmore East* and part way through *Eat a Peach*, Duane was killed in a motorcycle accident. A year later, original bassist Berry Oakley also died in a motorcycle crash near the site of Duane's tragic demise.

"Melissa" shows the folky, melodic side of the Allman Brothers Band at their peak. It was recorded after Duane's death and features Gregg on acoustic guitar and Dickey adding silky filigree with his trusty Les Paul.

Figure 29–Verses 1 and 2

The sixteen-measure verse is constructed around the intro chords. The parallel 4th movement along strings 4 and 5 create beautiful, lush voicings against the drone of the open B and E strings. Performance tip: Use a vigorous strumming motion directed from the elbow and let the strings ring out heartily as Gregg (Gtr. 2) did with his Martin.

Dickey (Gtr. 1) mostly plumbs the root position of the C♯ minor scale for his slinky fills. His choice of notes is pretty much based on feel with emphasis on the key center (E). In measure 7, he pulls a fast one by sustaining the A note over the A chord and the B note over the Bm chord. Likewise, in measures 8, 9, and 10, he emphasizes the root note of the changes. Though this is a very simple melodic concept, it's highly effective in light of the musical texture it creates.

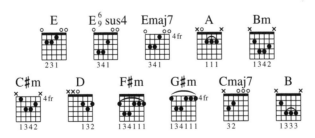

Fig. 29

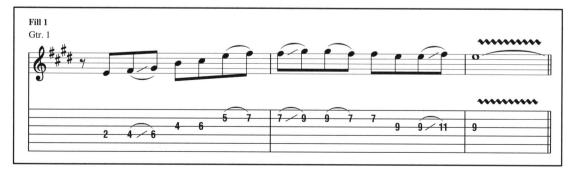

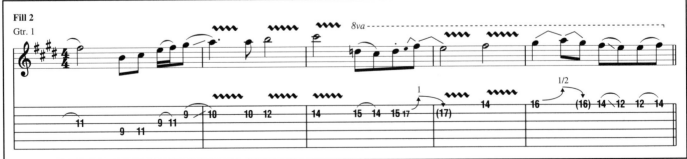

Figure 30–Coda

Starting in measure 4, Dickey solos over the intro chords repeated as a four-chord phrase. As the tonality very much centers around the I chord (E), he takes several opportunities to highlight the melodic 3rd (G♯), especially by bending up to it from F♯ (measures 3, 9, and 18). Like all great "modal" solos (one scale over many different chords), the secret to success is the sensitive balance between tension and release throughout. Both the root (E) and 3rd (G♯) notes function as points of resolution, with the 2nd or 9th (F♯) and 6th (C♯) degrees providing gentle musical tension. In measures 14, 15, and 16, he hammers and pulls between the A (4th) and G♯ (3rd) before sustaining the 5th (B) for a different (though stable) note of temporary resolution.

Dickey includes some blues sounds in measures 11 and 12, where he bends from the 9th (F♯) one half step to the ♭3rd or 10th (G) before releasing the bend back to the 9th and resolving to the root.

Performance tip: Whatever your choice of axe, use the neck pickup with a dollop of smooth distortion dialed in for a creamy, singing tone.

48 Full Band

49 Slow Demo
Gtr. 1

* volume swells

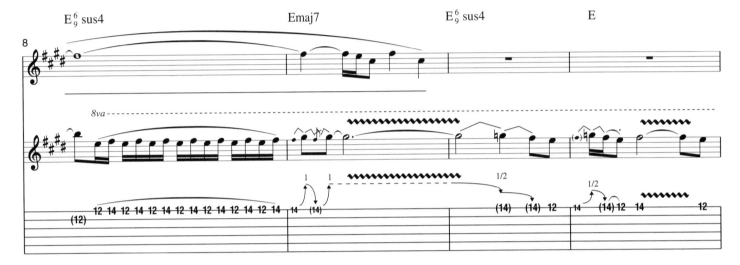

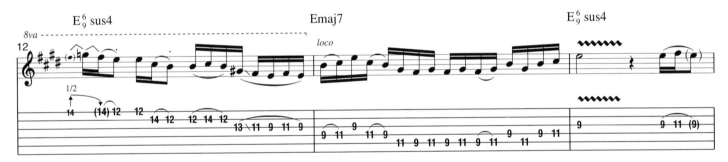

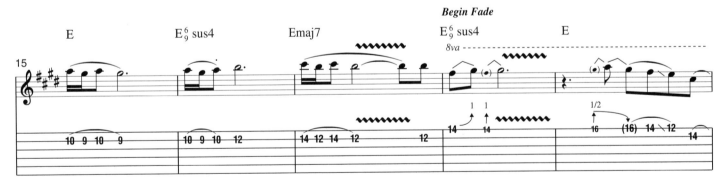

MISSISSIPPI QUEEN

Words and Music by Leslie West, Felix Pappalardi, Corky Laing and David Rea
Performed by Mountain on *Mountain Climbing* in 1970

If one accepts Southern rock as a genre based on style irrespective of locale or heritage, then Mountain fits in towards the heavy end of the scale—pun intended. Big Long Island, NY native Leslie West (*nee* Weinstein) got a tone as mammoth as his girth out of his Les Paul Junior (with a single P-90 pickup) and Marshall stack. As distinctive a signature sound as any rock guitarist of the era, his squeal made "Mississippi Queen" a blues-rock classic.

"Mississippi Queen" is a pile-driving I–IV–V rocker laced with some of the tastiest composite blues-scale licks and bends ever pawed over and squeezed. Though it was the one and only hit for Leslie West and Mountain, it was more than enough to insure the "Great Fatsby" (he has slimmed down considerably) immortality.

Figure 31–Intro

An insistent, clanging cowbell rings in a killer two-measure riff (Gtr. 1, Riff A) to kick off the ten-measure intro. Notice that the E basic blues scale position and the lick itself are reminiscent of the intro to "Purple Haze," as Hendrix was also an influence on West. Starting at the end of measure 6, West peals off a classic lick from the "B.B. King box" at the seventeenth position that bends the F♯ to the G♯ while sustaining the B to form the interval of a 3rd. Observe how the two-measure lick is played over both the V chord (B) and IV chord (A) changes. Concurrently, West begins the sliding two-measure barre chord and bass string pattern that underpins the I–IV–V chord progression.

Fig. 31

Intro

Half-time feel
Moderately ♩ = 140

Figure 32–Verse 1

The sixteen-measure verse functions like an extended I–IV vamp. It starts on the IV chord for four measures, followed by the I chord for four measures, and continues with the IV chord for an additional four measures. Measures 13–16 consist of a rest on the I chord followed by Riff A. Dig how West "answers" barre chords with a variety of licks that sometimes duplicate the root notes of the chords (measures 2, 6, 10, and 12). The cool half-step bends in each "answer" measure add juicy musical tension and resolve to the root note of the chord change.

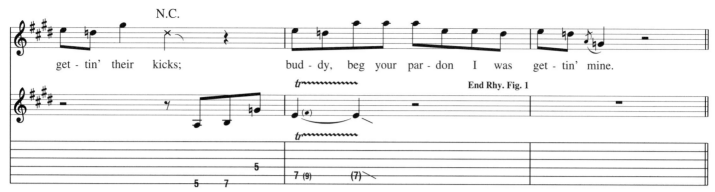

get - tin' their kicks; bud - dy, beg your par - don I was get - tin' mine.

Figure 33–Guitar Solo

West solos with serious blues attitude over the first nineteen of the twenty-nine measures that comprise the guitar solo and de facto coda. Measures 17–24 are like measures 9–16 of the verse inasmuch as they move V–IV–I and repeat the same lyrics. Over measures 24–29 West repeats Riff A three times. The last one ends on the tonic without the trill for final resolution.

Avoiding flash and fury in favor of taste, tone, and controlled technique, West bends and vibratos through several positions of the E composite blues scale with emphasis on the melodic 6th (C♯), 3rd (G♯), and 5th (B). Starting with his "theme" bend in the B.B. box, he seesaws back and forth between tension and release to the tonic note (E). Particularly noteworthy is the honking double-string bend (C/F♯ to C♯/G) in measures 7 and 8. The sweet and melodic repeated whole-step bend of B (5th) to C♯ (6th) in measures 15–18 leads smoothly to resolution on E in measure 19, thus putting the finishing touches on this well-crafted solo.

Fig. 33

52 Full Band

53 Slow Demo
Gtr. 2

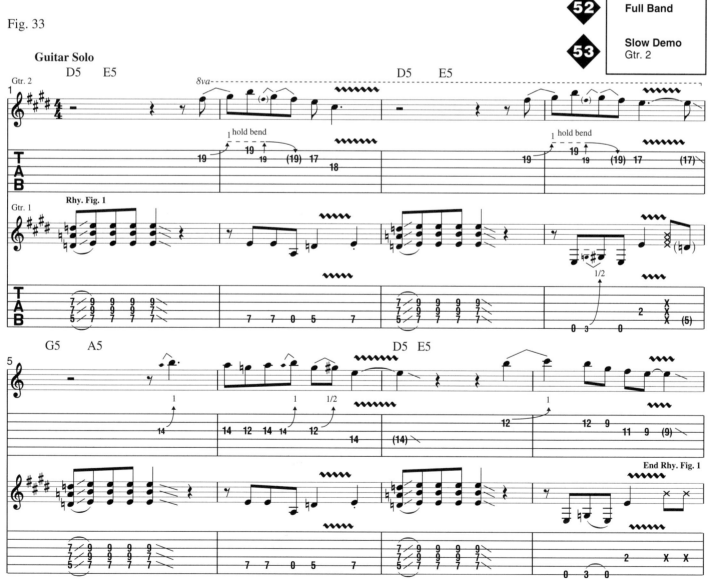

RAMBLIN' MAN

Words and Music by Dickey Betts
Performed by the Allman Brothers Band on _Brothers and Sisters_ in 1973

In 1973, Dickey Betts began to move out from under the massive shadow cast by the late Duane Allman with the release of _Brothers and Sisters_ and the #2 hit single "Ramblin' Man." In one fell swoop, he became the creative source for the band, writing, singing, and playing all the guitar parts. It must have been supremely satisfying to his ego to have this particular album shoot to #1 and become the Allman Brothers' most popular release. Additionally, the material reflected his personal interest in country music and was quite different from the heavy blues-rock that was Duane's legacy.

Betts scored yet another coup by getting a hit song on the radio that contained extended soloing as well as his signature harmony guitar—in this case overdubbed. The band was bigger than ever and poised to begin a new era. Unfortunately, the monolithic edifice they constructed showed signs of crumbling a year later as Betts and Gregg released solo albums, and relations among the band members grew strained. By 1976, the first breakup was underway.

Note: The recording is in G♯, necessitating the use of a capo at fret 1 or tuning up one half step.

Figure 34–Intro

Dickey Betts inhabits the E melodic minor scale throughout "Ramblin' Man." In the intro (Gtr. 1), he runs down from the extension to the root position at fret 12 in measures 1 and 2 before harmonizing with himself (Gtrs. 1 and 2) in measures 3 and 4. If you examine the tab closely, it reveals that one guitar could play these 3rds with some deft fingering. Try it. It's hip.

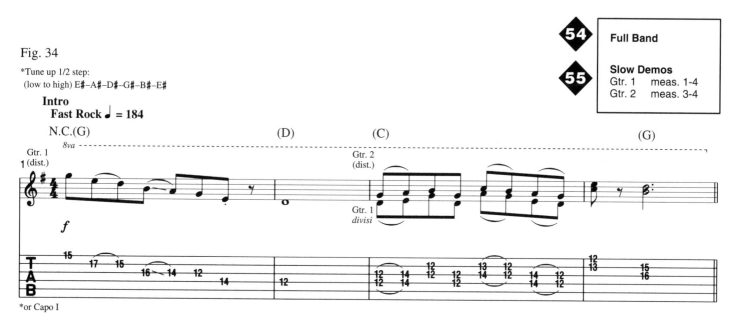

Fig. 34
*Tune up 1/2 step:
(low to high) E♯–A♯–D♯–G♯–B♯–E♯

Intro
Fast Rock ♩ = 184

N.C.(G)   (D)   (C)   (G)

Gtr. 1
1 (dist.)

*or Capo I

54 Full Band

55 Slow Demos
Gtr. 1   meas. 1–4
Gtr. 2   meas. 3–4

Figure 35–Chorus

The sixteen-measure chorus uses a combination of chords diatonic to the key of G with the addition of the ♭VII chord (F). Basic barre chord positions are employed with one notable exception: In measure 10, Betts plays a G derived from an open-position D chord. Moved up the neck to the seventh position with the 3rd (B) added on string 4, it connects gracefully to the Em triad in measure 11.

Fig. 35

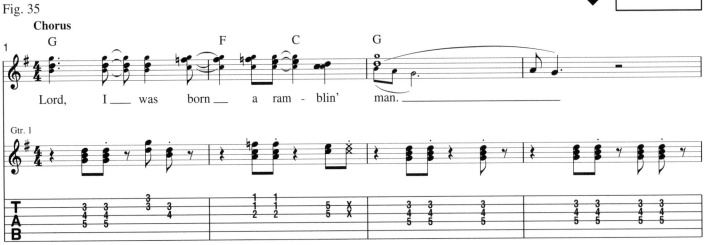

Lord, I ___ was born ___ a ram - blin' man. _____

Gtr. 1

Try'n to make a liv-ing, and do-in' the best I _____ can. An'

when it's time ___ for leav - in' ___ I hope you'll un - der - stand, _

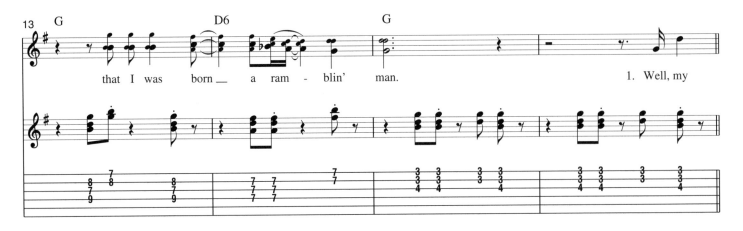

that I was born ___ a ram - blin' man. 1. Well, my

Figure 36–First 32 measures of Guitar Solo 2

Over a four-measure vamp (G, F–C, G, and G) Betts soars like a hawk, swooping and climbing his way through the E minor scale in several positions. Since the tonality is virtually completely focused on the tonic (I) chord, he continually resolves to the root (G) note after creating wave after wave of delightful musical tension. As a master improviser, he also "composes" as he goes along so that his solo builds magnificently. He locks into the B.B. King box around fret 8 and twirls many variations of the 2nd (A) bent to the melodic 3rd (B).

57 Full Band

58 Slow Demo
Gtr. 3

Fig. 36

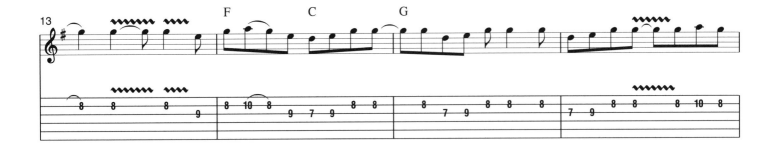

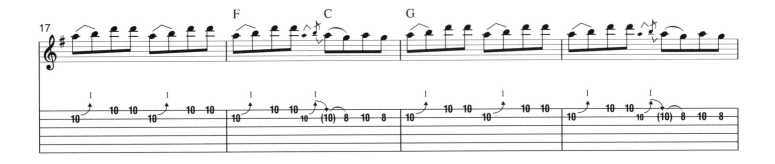

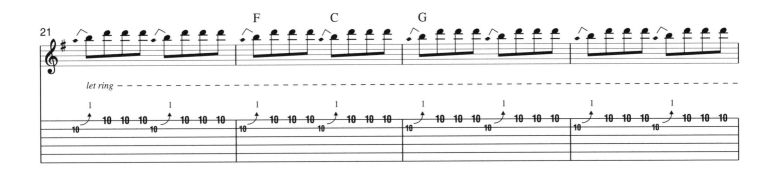

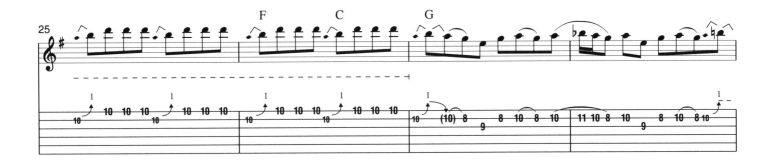

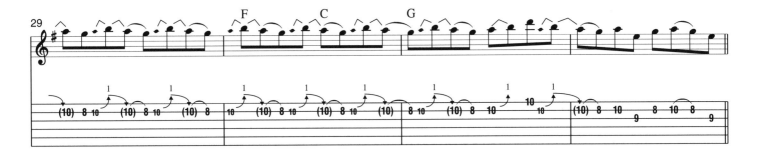

SO INTO YOU

Words and Music by Buddy Buie, Dean Daughtry and Robert Nix
Performed by Atlanta Rhythm Section on *A Rock and Roll Alternative* in 1976

The Atlanta Rhythm Section was formed in 1970 in Doraville, Georgia from the unlikely pairing of the remnants of the Classics IV and Roy Orbison's Candymen. The Classics IV, featuring the mellifluous vocals of frontman Dennis Yost, scored a number of catchy, soft-rock hits in the late sixties including "Stormy" and "Spooky." The Candymen, on the other hand, were particularly suited to the "Big O" and provided the appropriate rockabilly and ballad backup that he required. Surprisingly, the combination worked well, as the group carved their own niche out of the Southern rock genre with a style that was way more laid back, jazzier, and more melodic than most of their counterparts.

After treading water for five years, the ARS broke through with *A Rock and Roll Alternative* (#11) and the hit single "So Into You" (#7) in 1976. The album went gold, which, along with their constant touring, gave them credibility on FM radio and in concert.

"So Into You" is based on i–iv-v minor key changes and contains the trademark electric piano and guitar harmonies that made the Atlanta Rhythm Section so appealing to listeners beyond Southern rock fans. Along with Barry Bailey's fleet-fingered runs and the band's lilting funk rhythms, ARS contributed to an enduring quality besides the obvious nostalgia for a golden age of rock guitar.

Figure 37–Verse 1

Gtrs. 1 and 2 divide the fingerboard between the upper and lower registers for a full-spectrum sound. Observe the cool alternate voicing of the Fm7 (following the root-position form) played by Gtr. 2 in measures 4. It is also interesting to note how measures 1–8 follow a 12-bar blues arrangement but then deviate. Measure 9 contains the i chord, though it's altered (Fm7sus4) and continues into beats 1 and 2 of measure 10, with beats 3 and 4 moving to the v (Cm7). Measure 11, in 2/4 time, serves as a pickup into the chorus that follows.

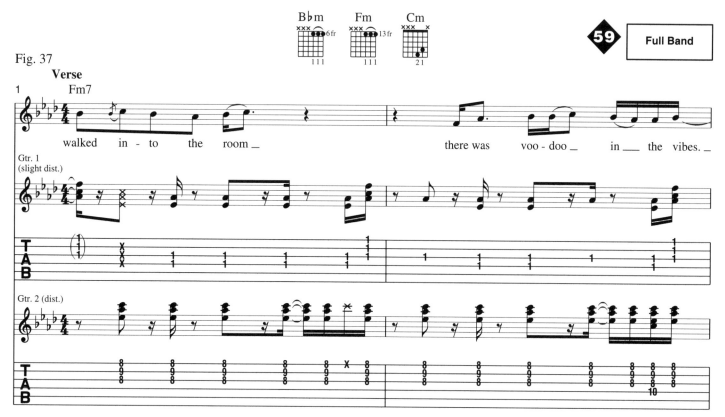

I was cap - tured by your style,

but I could _ not catch your eyes. _____ Now I stand _

here _____ help-less - ly _____ hop-ing you'll _ get in - to _____ me. I am

Figure 38–Bridge

The ten-measure instrumental bridge vamps between the iv and i chords for two measures each. Dig the ultra-cool three-part harmony in measures 1–8 (two four-measure phrases), with Gtr. 1 playing the melody from the F Aeolian mode. Check out how the two chord changes are acknowledged simply and effectively by ending the phrase on a different strategic note each time. In addition, check out the resolution to the root (F) in measures 3 and 4. The sound produced is so creamy and smooth that it recalls nothing less than the Glenn Miller Orchestra in its prime playing "Moonlight Serenade." Notice how the bass run and the comping in measures 9 and 10 function as a pickup and an intro into verse 2 (not shown).

Performance tip: With two guitars, one plays the melody of Gtr. 1, and the other should play the harmony of Gtr. 3.

Figure 39–Outro Solo

Moving seamlessly from the chorus into the outro solo, the band vamps iv–i while Bailey (Gtr. 1) skims along smooth as glass in the F minor pentatonic scale with his fat Les Paul. After having noodled (albeit artfully) on frets 13 and 15 of the third string, he finally gives into the blues side of his personality and burns in the octave root position at fret 13 with a blur of thirty-second notes in measures 3 and 5. The twisting three-note repeating riff in measure 9 jacks up the energy a tad as the tune fades. As opposed to the bridge, the object here is to convey expressive waves of tension and release (usually to the F) not necessarily tied to the actual chord change.

Fig. 39

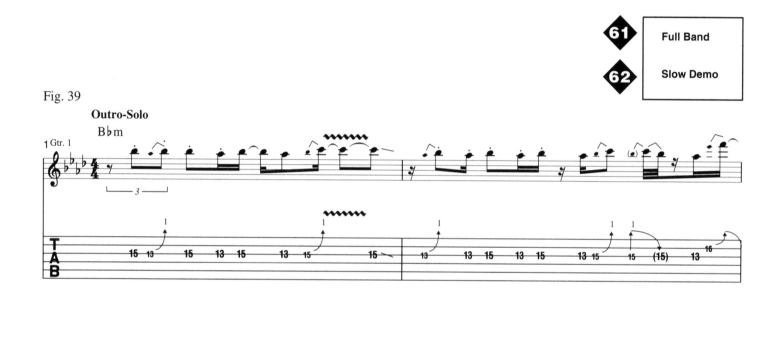

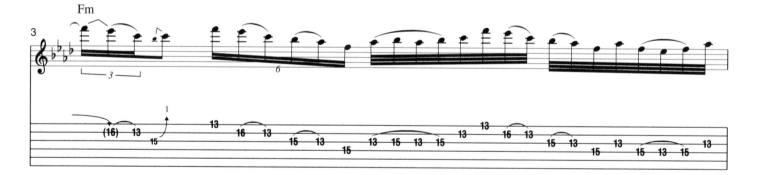

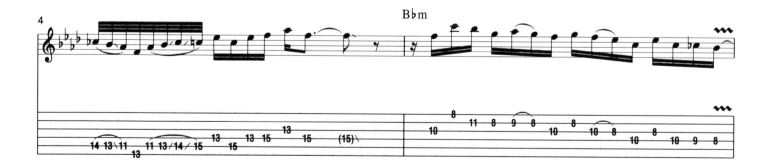

Begin fade

Fade out

STATESBORO BLUES

Word and Music by Willy McTell
Performed by the Allman Brothers Band on *Live at Fillmore East* **in 1971**

The Brothers had more than demonstrated blues credentials on their first album, but they blew away all doubt with their classic live set. One of the highlights on that album, besides their epic version of "Stormy Monday," was their amazing shuffle arrangement of Blind Willie McTell's "Statesboro Blues." The original 1929 recording featured McTell paying tribute to his hometown in Georgia while swinging along on the acoustic 12-string guitar in the same key (D) as the ABB.

"Statesboro Blues" is a first-rate showcase for virtually everyone in the band, from the pumping rhythm section, to Brother Greg's blues-approved vocals, to the outstanding guitar work of Duane and Dickey. Allman's slide playing was never more confident, emitting tone akin to an alto saxophone. Betts, on the other hand (pun intended!), proves himself every bit as qualified for his position, peeling off a melodic and memorable fretted solo that soars as high as "Sky Dog's" on this 12-bar classic. Without question, this is one of the greatest performances in the history of blues guitar.

Figure 40–Intro

Gtr. 1 (Allman) and Gtr. 2 (Betts) play a classic blues stop-time riff of the 5th (A) to the ♭7th (C), resolving to the root (D) in unison to signal the commencement of the tune. Alternating every other measure with the riff, or "call," is Duane's "response" of sassy slide fills. He phrases behind the beat like the true bluesman he was, drawing out sustained and watery vibratoed notes in a sensuous display of tantalizing musical tension.

Starting in measure 9 the band kicks in with Betts playing a basic boogie accompaniment (Rhy. Fig.1) that girds the I–IV–V changes throughout "Statesboro Blues." Dig how Allman masterfully presents wave after wave of tension and release over the I–IV (D–G) chords in measures 9–16. In measure 17, he marks the V chord change with the root (A) and melodic 6th (F♯) notes. He then winds up his intro solo with a snappy improvised turnaround (measures 19 and 20) that resolves to the root (A) of the V chord.

63 Full Band

64 Slow Demo
Gtr. 1

Fig. 40

Gtr. 1: Open E Tuning:
(low to high) E–B–E–G♯–B–E

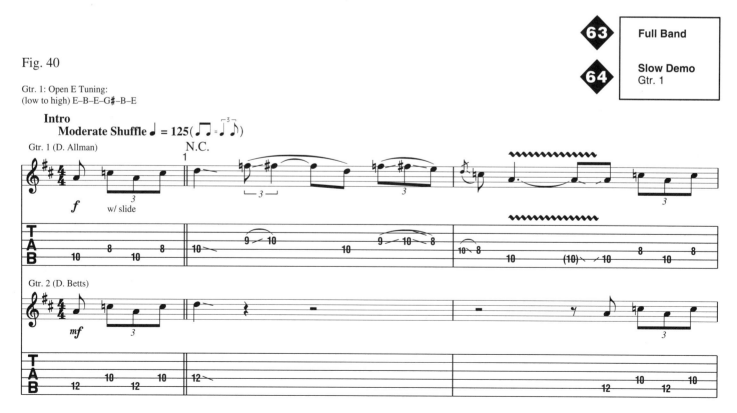

*Chord symbols outline general harmony throughout.

**Slide positioned halfway between 13th and 14th fret.

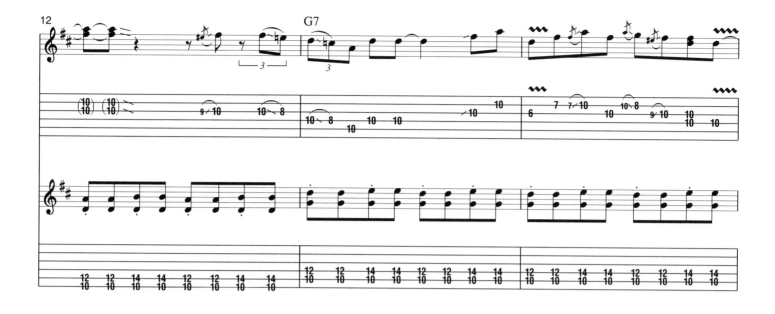

Figure 41–Guitar Solo 1 (Duane)

Duane's approach to following the changes in "Statesboro Blues" is to mainly play combinations of the root (D) and major 3rd (F♯) over the I chord and the 5th (D) with the occasional root (G) over the IV chord. For the V chord, he favors emphasis on the root. Like his intro solo and fills, Duane plays mostly in the root position of D around fret 10, as did Elmore James, the "king" of open D tuning. Be sure to check out his use of the ♭3rd (F) as a grace note before the major 3rd (F♯) in measures 4 and 7.

In chorus 2 of his twenty-four-measure solo, Duane glides up to the octave around fret 22 and cruises in the stratosphere without diminishing accuracy, intonation, or note selection. Keeping the gas on high, he maintains his position in the upper register and plays a series of slashing triplets in measures 21 and 22. He even completes his turn-around in place before *quickly* dropping to the tenth position to play the unison riff with Dickey as a pickup to verse 3, thus ending his virtuosic performance with a flourish and throwing the gauntlet down for Dickey.

65 Full Band

66 Slow Demo
Gtr. 1

Fig. 41

Guitar Solo (D.A.)

Gtr. 2: w/ Rhy. Fig. 1

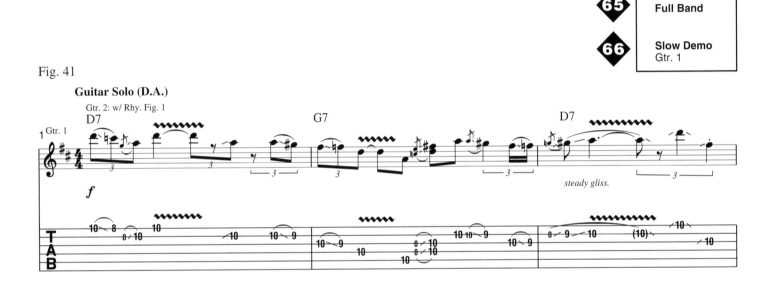

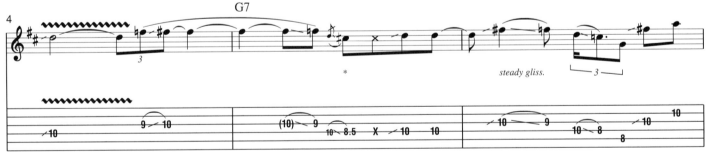

*Slide positioned halfway between 8th and 9th fret.

Figure 42–Guitar Solo 2 (Dickey)

Dickey Betts graciously (?) stood in the shadows of Duane's legendary stature for years, yet in reality, he could certainly hold his own in a shootout. When his turn to shine comes in "Statesboro Blues," he radiates heat and light with a melodic solo constructed around the B blues scale (relative to D major). As would be expected, he emphasizes the major 3rd (F♯), especially over the I chord, and the sweet 6th (B) notes. Observe how Dickey builds his solo similarly to Duane's, beginning in the root position of the B blues scale at fret 7 (measures 1–4) and relocating to the B.B. King box around fret 15 until the end of his first twelve-bar segment. The bending lick in measures 8 and 9 (E bent to F♯ on string 2, combined with A on string 1) was one of Dickey's trademarks, most prominently showcased on "Ramblin' Man."

In chorus 2 of his twenty-four-measure solo, Dickey drops in briefly on the root position of the D basic blues scale at fret 10 before finding a home in the Albert King box around fret 13 for the remainder of his ride. With the main emphasis on the D note, he works in a series of half- and full-step bends from the G note at fret 15 on string 1. Played over all three chord changes, these bends provide a wealth of hip harmony with 5ths (A) and ♭5ths (G♯) over the D, 9ths (A) and ♭9ths (A♭) over the G, and the root (A) as resolution over the A. Dickey wraps up his solo with the same chromatic sequence in measures 23 and 24 that he played in measures 11 and 12, only one octave higher—cool!

67   **Full Band**

68   **Slow Demo**
       Gtr. 2

Fig. 42

Guitar Solo (D.B.)

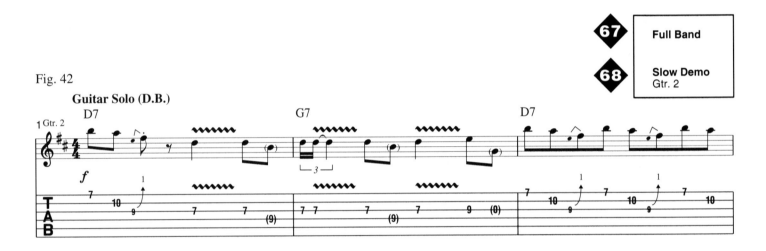

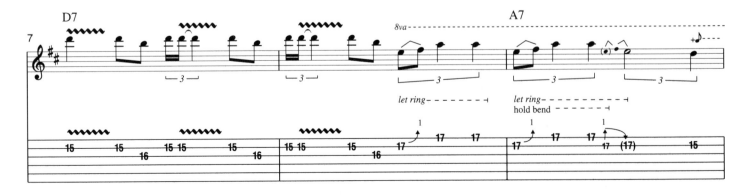

76

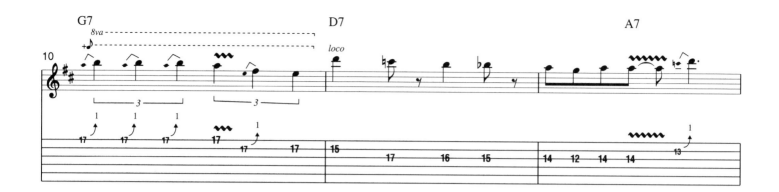

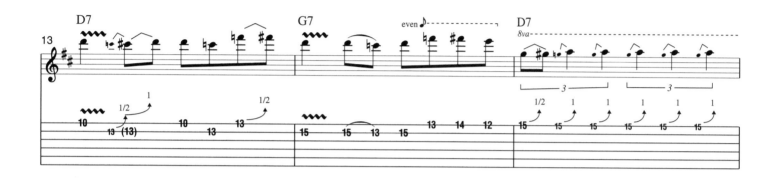

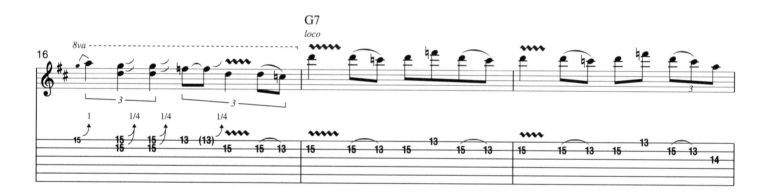

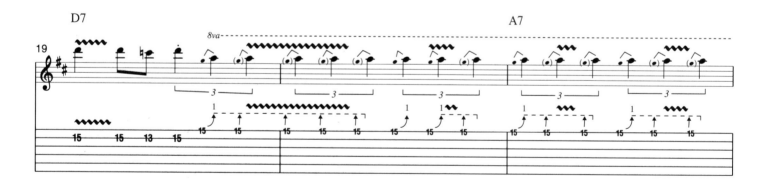

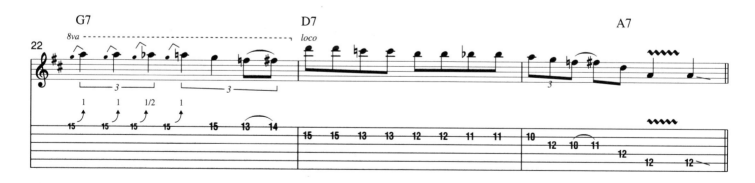

SUSIE-Q

Words and Music by Dale Hawkins, Stan Lewis and Eleanor Broadwater
Performed by Creedence Clearwater Revival in 1968

If you had set out in the late sixties to create the perfect American rock band by combining blues, country, and folk influences with contemporary psychedelic elements into 3:00 minute pop classics, the result would have been Creedence Clearwater Revival. From 1968 to 1971, they ruled Top 40 radio stateside in a similar if less overwhelming way than the Beatles did in the previous five years. With the multitalented John Fogerty at the helm, his brother Tom on rhythm guitar, and the solid backbone of bassist Stu Cook and drummer Doug Clifford, Creedence Clearwater Revival epitomized the spirit of rootsy rock 'n' roll.

Though CCR formed in 1967 in Cerrito, California, they existed in various incarnations during the late fifties and early sixties as the Blue Velvets and the Golliwogs. It was not until John rose to take command of all creative aspects as frontman that the potential of the group was realized. With a new and hipper name, they released their self-titled debut album in 1968. Included was the epic, extended psychedelic version of Dale Hawkins' 1957 rockabilly classic, "Susie-Q." Trimmed for radio play, it peaked at #16. The band's breakthrough occurred with their sophomore effort in 1969, however, as *Bayou Country* not only contained "Born on the Bayou" (Fogerty had not been further south than Southern California at this point!) but the #1 "Proud Mary" as well. The fact that it has since become a wedding band staple by no means detracts from its timeless quality and superb craftsmanship. No less an authority on authentic folk music than Bob Dylan gave it his enthusiastic imprimatur.

For the next two years, the hit singles kept coming, as "Bad Moon Rising," "Green River," "Down on the Corner," "Travelin' Band," "Who'll Stop the Rain," "Up Around the Bend," "Long As I Can See the Light," and "Have You Ever Seen the Rain?" all stormed up the charts. In addition, John let his political views on Vietnam show with "Fortunate Son" and "Run Through the Jungle." In the guitar freak-out tradition of "Susie-Q" and "I Put a Spell on You," he also covered "I Heard It Through the Grapevine."

Despite the band's runaway success, self-destructive dissention within the group led to Tom Fogerty splitting in 1971 for an undistinguished solo career. Doug Clifford and Stu Cook lobbied for equal shares of the songwriting and singing, resulting in the disappointing *Mardi Gras* in 1972—CCR's swan song. On top of the acrimonious breakup, there followed years of debilitating litigation between John and Fantasy Records over the rights to his songs.

In 1973, John put out an album of cover tunes as the Blue Ridge Rangers, followed by *John Fogerty* in 1975—both to little acclaim. After a hiatus, he made a significant comeback with *Centerfield* in 1984, but *Eye of the Zombie* in 1986 was less successful. After another lengthy layoff, he resurfaced once again in 1997 with *Blue Moon Swamp* followed by the live *Premonition* in 1998. In the meantime, any hopes of a CCR "revival" were dashed when his brother Tom died in 1990. As for Clifford and Cook, they went out as a CCR cover band called Creedence Clearwater Revisited in 1995 with Elliot Easton on guitar and John Tristao on vocals. The double CD of their classics was quashed, however, by Fogerty's competing Premonition, which contained similar material.

"Susie-Q, Pt. 1" is basically a i chord (Em) vamp with a release to the IV, ♭III, and V chords. It grooves relentlessly and is highlighted by John's two squawking guitar solos that clearly display his bluesy, soulful touch and funky midrange tone (perhaps played on a Rickenbacker 325 model). He was also fond of using a Gibson Les Paul Custom and a Dobro with CCR.

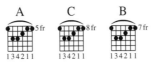

Figure 43–Intro

The intro comes diddly-bopping in with the swampy open-position licks that John repeats throughout. Virtually identical to the legendary James Burton's picking on the Dale Hawkins original, it resembles a backwards version of Willie Johnson's signature lick on Howlin' Wolf's "Moanin' at Midnight" from 1951. In its own way, it's a classic descending blues run. Beginning with the ♭7th (D), it makes its way down the E minor pentatonic scale, concluding with a bluesy bend from G (♭3rd) to G♯ (3rd).

Brother Tom (Gtr. 2) chunks along behind John with a signature Creedence pattern (Rhy. Fig. 1). The root note on the low E is punctuated by first the E major and its corresponding E7 voicing at fret 7. Both "Born on the Bayou" and "Keep on Chooglin'" have similar accompaniments.

Figure 44–Verse

The sixteen-measure verse is comprised of two eight-measure sections. John simplifies his E riff, creating a "call and response" pattern between his vocal line and guitar in measures 1–4. He chanks big, six-string barre chords (A, C, and B) on the backbeats in measures 5 and 6 and returns to the modified E riff in measures 7 and 8. Observe that Tom just plays the root bass notes under the chords, always being the supportive rhythm man.

CCR were the masters of the "locked-in groove," and nowhere is this more clearly presented than in the verse of "Susie-Q." These flannel-shirted hippies lived for the "2" and "4." Not to be overlooked are the contributions of Clifford and Cook, who simmer at a low boil behind the Fogerty brothers. Perhaps it's John's passion for baseball that compelled the band members to be such consummate team players.

70 Full Band

Figure 45–Guitar Solo 1

John Fogerty is no virtuoso, but the man sure knows how to get to the emotional center of a solo quickly and milk it for all its worth. His solo is played over the verse chord changes. With the root-octave position of the E minor pentatonic scale as his sole improvising tool, he mainly wrenches the 4th (A) up to the 5th (B) with eventual resolution to the root (E) note. Measures 1 and 2, however, contain a tasty bend of the root to the 2nd (F#) on string 4, using wicked vibrato for a robust sound and a bold entrance. Like all great guitarists facing a modal situation, he intuitively knows how to compose wave after wave of tension and release. He climaxes his solo by repeating the 4th-to-5th bend on every beat in measure 13 after previewing the effect in measure 10. In addition, even though his guitar does not possess much sustain, his tone is loaded with midrange harmonics that respond well to his touch with the pick.

Fig. 45

THUNDERBIRD

By Walter Jacobs
Performed by ZZ Top on *Fandango* in 1975

Long before they became hairy MTV idols, guitarist Billy Gibbons, bassist Dusty Hill, and drummer Frank Beard were the hardest rocking little blues trio to come out of Texas. Possessing exceptional chops and deep-rooted feel that belied their wry sense of humor, the Top brought the healing power of the blues to the radio waves in the seventies. Muscling aside the weepy, sensitive singer/songwriters and fatuous glam-rockers of the era, they boogied their way into the public consciousness, laying the groundwork for Stevie Ray Vaughan and the second Blues Revival in the eighties. Ironically, Gibbons & Co. opted to go for the bucks with a screeching right hand turn to pop music at that point, but as John Lee Hooker once said, "When you got that boogie in you, it's got to come out." No less an authority than Jimi Hendrix named Gibbons (who had opened for the Experience while still in the Moving Sidewalks) his favorite guitarist while chatting with Johnny Carson on the "Tonight Show."

"Thunderbird" is ZZ Top's version of Little Walter's paean to cheap Thunderbird wine via a 12-bar blues rave-up. Recorded live at the Warehouse in New Orleans, it confirms the utter superiority that Gibbons' blues guitar playing could exhibit if only he took it as seriously as Stevie Ray Vaughan—or even Eric Clapton, for that matter.

Figure 46–Chorus

Through measures 1–8, Gibbons plays driving boogie patterns employing 5ths and 6ths for the I (C) and IV (F) chords. In measures 9 and 10 (V and IV), however, he inserts major barre chords to pump up the overall sound before the turnaround in measures 11 and 12. Observe how Gibbons plays the typical Robert Johnson-type descending turnaround pattern in measure 11 and then reverses direction in measure 12 in order to maintain the tune's button-popping momentum. Dig the "shorthand" C/G (root/5th) double stop on beat 4 of measure 12 to identify the V chord (G).

Performance tip: Use even down and up strokes for the boogie patterns in order to keep up with the blistering (no joke!) tempo.

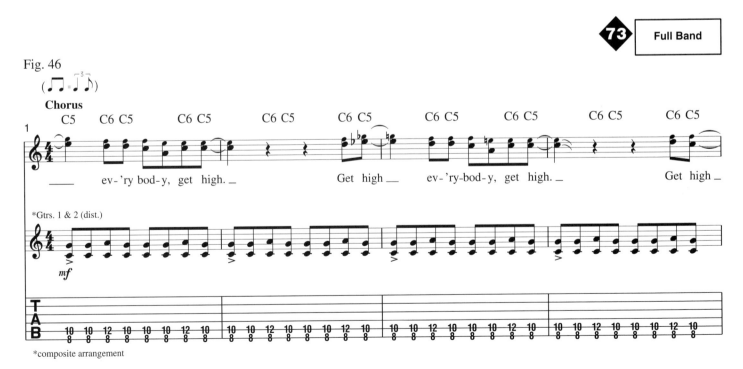

Fig. 46

Figure 47–Guitar Solo

Gibbons rocks the house with three honking choruses of Les Paul-powered, blues guitar deluxe soloing that just drips with rich, harmonic distortion. With the root position of the C blues scale at fret 8 as his basis, he also includes the extension position between frets 11 and 13 and the next lowest "box" between frets 6 and 8 on string 5. He builds the tension beautifully and incrementally in each chorus, moving up the fingerboard from the root position to the extension and culminating in double stops to cap his relentlessly swinging aural assault on the senses. Though he does not follow the changes religiously in each and every measure, Gibbons emphasizes enough signposts along the way to insure harmonic integrity. In chorus 1, it's evident in the root (G) over the V in measure 9 along with the root (F) bent a full step and released in measure 10 (IV). In chorus 2, he leans heavily on the root (C) in measures 13–16 in addition to the major 3rd (E) and cool, melodic 6th (A).

Chorus 3 is the hippest, however. Gibbons repeats B♭/G (7th/♭5th) over the I chord in measures 25–28, moving the same formation up the neck two frets to C/A (5th/3rd) for the IV chord in measures 29 and 30. The note selection emphasizes the chord changes conclusively, while the repetition of the triplets creates wonderful tension. One antecedent for this slick trick can be found in Chuck Berry's solo in "No Particular Place to Go," while yet another example of this concept is heard in George Thorogood's version of the Hank Williams classic "Move It on Over."

74 Full Band

75 Slow Demo

Fig. 44

Guitar Solo

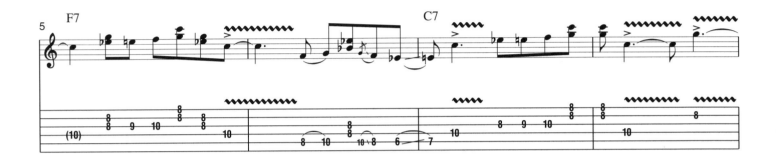

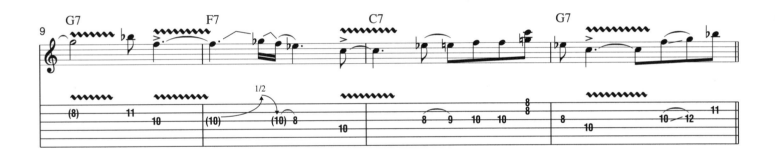

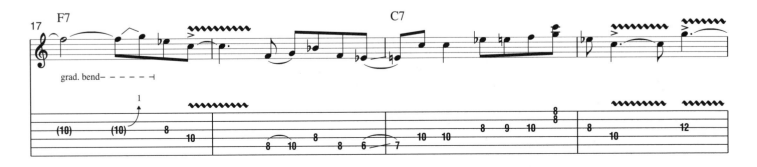

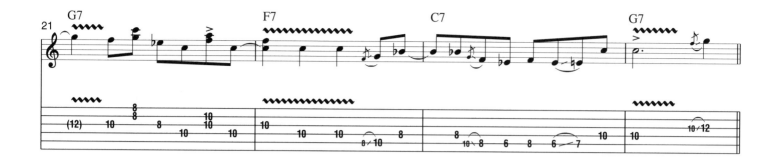

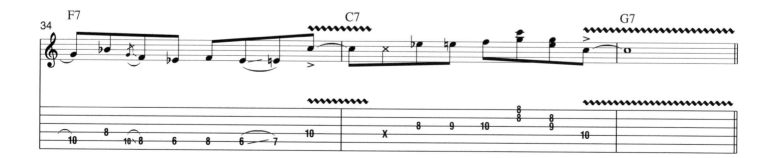

Guitar Notation Legend

Guitar Music can be notated three different ways: on a *musical staff*, in *tablature*, and in *rhythm slashes*.

RHYTHM SLASHES are written above the staff. Strum chords in the rhythm indicated. Use the chord diagrams found at the top of the first page of the transcription for the appropriate chord voicings. Round noteheads indicate single notes.

THE MUSICAL STAFF shows pitches and rhythms and is divided by bar lines into measures. Pitches are named after the first seven letters of the alphabet.

TABLATURE graphically represents the guitar fingerboard. Each horizontal line represents a string, and each number represents a fret.

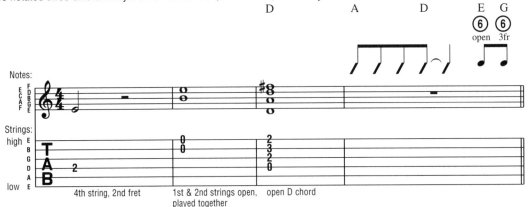

4th string, 2nd fret   1st & 2nd strings open, played together   open D chord

HALF-STEP BEND: Strike the note and bend up 1/2 step.

WHOLE-STEP BEND: Strike the note and bend up one step.

GRACE NOTE BEND: Strike the note and immediately bend up as indicated.

SLIGHT (MICROTONE) BEND: Strike the note and bend up 1/4 step.

BEND AND RELEASE: Strike the note and bend up as indicated, then release back to the original note. Only the first note is struck.

PRE-BEND: Bend the note as indicated, then strike it.

VIBRATO: The string is vibrated by rapidly bending and releasing the note with the fretting hand.

WIDE VIBRATO: The pitch is varied to a greater degree by vibrating with the fretting hand.

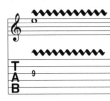

HAMMER-ON: Strike the first (lower) note with one finger, then sound the higher note (on the same string) with another finger by fretting it without picking.

PULL-OFF: Place both fingers on the notes to be sounded. Strike the first note and without picking, pull the finger off to sound the second (lower) note.

LEGATO SLIDE: Strike the first note and then slide the same fret-hand finger up or down to the second note. The second note is not struck.

SHIFT SLIDE: Same as legato slide, except the second note is struck.

TRILL: Very rapidly alternate between the notes indicated by continuously hammering on and pulling off.

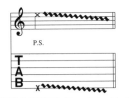

TAPPING: Hammer ("tap") the fret indicated with the pick-hand index or middle finger and pull off to the note fretted by the fret hand.

NATURAL HARMONIC: Strike the note while the fret-hand lightly touches the string directly over the fret indicated.

PINCH HARMONIC: The note is fretted normally and a harmonic is produced by adding the edge of the thumb or the tip of the index finger of the pick hand to the normal pick attack.

PICK SCRAPE: The edge of the pick is rubbed down (or up) the string, producing a scratchy sound.

MUFFLED STRINGS: A percussive sound is produced by laying the fret hand across the string(s) without depressing, and striking them with the pick hand.

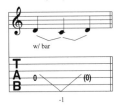

PALM MUTING: The note is partially muted by the pick hand lightly touching the string(s) just before the bridge.

RAKE: Drag the pick across the strings indicated with a single motion.

TREMOLO PICKING: The note is picked as rapidly and continuously as possible.

VIBRATO BAR DIVE AND RETURN: The pitch of the note or chord is dropped a specified number of steps (in rhythm) then returned to the original pitch.

VIBRATO BAR SCOOP: Depress the bar just before striking the note, then quickly release the bar.

VIBRATO BAR DIP: Strike the note and then immediately drop a specified number of steps, then release back to the original pitch.

GUITAR *signature licks*

Signature Licks book/CD packs provide a step-by-step breakdown of "right from the record" riffs, licks, and solos so you can jam along with your favorite bands. They contain full performance notes and an overview of each artist or group's style, with note-for-note transcriptions in notes and tab. The CDs feature full-band demos at both normal and slow speeds.

ACOUSTIC GUITAR OF '60S AND '70S
00695024 Book/CD Pack $19.95

ACOUSTIC GUITAR OF '80S AND '90S
00695033 Book/CD Pack $19.95

AEROSMITH 1973-1979
00695106 Book/CD Pack..........$19.95

AEROSMITH 1979-1998
00695219 Book/CD Pack $19.95

BEATLES BASS
00695283 Book/CD Pack $19.95

THE BEATLES FAVORITES
00695096 Book/CD Pack $19.95

THE BEATLES HITS
00695049 Book/CD Pack $19.95

BEST OF THE BEATLES FOR ACOUSTIC GUITAR
00695453 Book/CD Pack..........$19.95

BEST OF GEORGE BENSON
00695418 Book/CD Pack..........$19.95

THE BEST OF BLACK SABBATH
00695249 Book/CD Pack $19.95

BEST OF AGGRO-METAL
00695592 Book/CD Pack $19.95

BEST OF JAZZ GUITAR
00695586 Book/CD Pack $24.95

BEST OF R&B
00695288 Book/CD Pack..........$19.95

BEST OF ROCK 'N' ROLL GUITAR
00695559 Book/CD Pack $19.95

BLUES GUITAR CLASSICS
00695177 Book/CD Pack $19.95

THE BEST OF ERIC CLAPTON
00695038 Book/CD Pack $24.95

ERIC CLAPTON – THE BLUESMAN
00695040 Book/CD Pack $19.95

ERIC CLAPTON – FROM THE ALBUM UNPLUGGED
00695250 Book/CD Pack $19.95

THE BEST OF CREAM
00695251 Book/CD Pack $19.95

BEST OF DEEP PURPLE
00695625 Book/CD Pack $19.95

THE BEST OF DEF LEPPARD
00696516 Book/CD Pack $19.95

THE DOORS
00695373 Book/CD Pack $19.95

BEST OF FOO FIGHTERS
00695481 Book/CD Pack......$19.95

GREATEST GUITAR SOLOS OF ALL TIME
00695301 Book/CD Pack..........$19.95

GUITAR INSTRUMENTAL HITS
00695309 Book/CD Pack..........$17.95

GUITAR RIFFS OF THE '60S
00695218 Book/CD pack..........$17.95

GUITAR RIFFS OF THE '70S
00695158 Book/CD Pack $17.95

THE BEST OF GUNS N' ROSES
00695183 Book/CD Pack..........$19.95

THE BEST OF BUDDY GUY
00695186 Book/CD Pack..........$19.95

JIMI HENDRIX
00696560 Book/CD Pack $22.95

ERIC JOHNSON
00699317 Book/CD Pack $19.95

ROBERT JOHNSON
00695264 Book/CD Pack..........$19.95

B.B. KING – THE DEFINITIVE COLLECTION
00695635 Book/CD Pack $19.95

MARK KNOPFLER
00695178 Book/CD Pack..........$19.95

MEGADETH
00695041 Book/CD Pack $19.95

WES MONTGOMERY
00695387 Book/CD Pack..........$19.95

MOTOWN BASS
00695506 Book/CD Pack $16.95

PINK FLOYD – EARLY CLASSICS
00695566 Book/CD Pack..........$19.95

THE GUITARS OF ELVIS
00696507 Book/CD Pack..........$19.95

BEST OF QUEEN
00695097 Book/CD Pack $19.95

BEST OF RAGE AGAINST THE MACHINE
00695480 Book/CD Pack $19.95

THE RED HOT CHILI PEPPERS
00695173 Book/CD Pack $19.95

THE BEST OF THE RED HOT CHILI PEPPERS FOR BASS
00695285 Book/CD Pack $19.95

THE ROLLING STONES
00695079 Book/CD Pack..........$19.95

THE BEST OF JOE SATRIANI
00695216 Book/CD Pack $19.95

BEST OF SILVERCHAIR
00695488 Book/CDPack $19.95

STEVE VAI
00673247 Book/CD Pack $22.95

STEVE VAI – ALIEN LOVE SECRETS: THE NAKED VAMPS
00695223 Book/CD Pack..........$19.95

STEVE VAI – FIRE GARDEN: THE NAKED VAMPS
00695166 Book/CD Pack..........$19.95

STEVIE RAY VAUGHAN
00699316 Book/CD Pack $19.95

THE GUITAR STYLE OF STEVIE RAY VAUGHAN
00695155 Book/CD Pack $19.95

THE WHO
00695561 Book/CD Pack..........$19.95

GET BETTER AT GUITAR

...with These Great Guitar Instruction Books from Hal Leonard!

DON'T FRET NOTE MAP
REVOLUTIONARY GUITAR FINGER POSITIONING GUIDE
• *created by Nicholas Ravagni*

It's never been easier to learn to play guitar! For beginners just starting out or experienced guitarists who want to learn to read music, the *Don't Fret Note Map™* will give players the tools they need to locate notes on the guitar. This revolutionary finger positioning guide fits all electric and acoustic guitars with no adhesive or fasteners, shows the note names and locations all over the fretboard and uses a unique color-coded method to make note-reading easy. The accompanying booklet includes full instructions and four easy songs to let players practice their new-found skills!
_____00695587 ....$9.95

Also available:
DON'T FRET CHORD MAP™
REVOLUTIONARY GUITAR FINGER POSITIONING GUIDE
• *created by Nicholas Ravagni*
_____00695670 ....$9.95

GUITAR DIAL 9-1-1
50 WAYS TO IMPROVE YOUR PLAYING ... Now!! • *by Ken Parille*

Need to breathe new life into your guitar playing? This book is your admission into the Guitar ER! You'll learn to: expand your harmonic vocabulary; improvise with chromatic notes; create rhythmic diversity; improve your agility through helpful drills; supply soulful fills; create melodic lines through chord changes; and much more! The accompanying CD includes 99 demonstration tracks.
_____00695405 Book/CD Pack.................................$16.95

GUITAR TECHNIQUES • *by Michael Mueller*
Guitar Techniques is a terrific reference and teaching companion, as it clearly defines and demonstrates how to properly execute cool moves ranging from bending, vibrato and legato to tapping, whammy bar and playing with your teeth! The CD contains 92 demonstration tracks in country, rock, pop and jazz styles. Essential techniques covered include: Fretting • Strumming • Trills • Picking • Vibrato • Tapping • Bends • Harmonics • Muting • Slides • and more.
_____00695562 Book/CD Pack.................................$14.95

THE GUITARIST'S SURVIVAL KIT
EVERYTHING YOU NEED TO KNOW TO BE A WORKING MUSICIAN
• *by Dale Turner*

From repertoire to accompaniment patterns to licks, this book is fully stocked to give you the confidence knowing you can "get by" and survive, regardless of the situation. The book covers: songs and set lists; gear; rhythm riffs in styles from blues to funk to rock to metal; lead licks in blues, country, jazz & rock styles; transposition and more. The CD features 99 demonstration tracks, and the book includes standard notation and tab.
_____00695380 Book/CD Pack.................................$14.95

LEFT-HANDED GUITAR
THE COMPLETE METHOD • *by Troy Stetina*

Attention all Southpaws: it's time to turn your playing around! We're proud to announce that our groundbreaking guitar method solely devoted to lefties is now available with a CD! Complete with photos, diagrams and grids designed especially for the left-handed player, this book/CD pack teaches fundamentals such as: chords, scales, riffs, strumming; rock, blues, fingerpicking and other styles; tuning and theory; reading standard notation and tablature; and much more!
_____00695630 Book/CD Pack....................................$14.95
_____00695247 Book Only..$9.95

PICTURE CHORD ENCYCLOPEDIA
PHOTOS & DIAGRAMS FOR 2,600 GUITAR CHORDS!

The most comprehensive guitar chord resource ever! Beginning with helpful notes on how to use the book, how to choose the best voicings and how to construct chords, this extensive, 272-page source for all playing styles and levels features five easy-to-play voicings of 44 chord qualities for each of the twelve musical keys – 2,640 chords in all! For each, there is a clearly illustrated chord frame, as well as *an actual photo* of the chord being played! Includes info on basic fingering principles, open chords and barre chords, partial chords and broken-set forms, and more. Great for all guitarists!
_____00695224 ....$19.95

SCALE CHORD RELATIONSHIPS
A GUIDE TO KNOWING WHAT NOTES TO PLAY – AND WHY!
• *by Michael Mueller & Jeff Schroedl*

Scale Chord Relationships teaches players how to determine which scales to play with which chords, so guitarists will never have to fear chord changes again! This book/CD pack explains how to: recognize keys; analyze chord progressions; use the modes; play over nondiatonic harmony; use harmonic and melodic minor scales; use symmetrical scales such as chromatic, whole-tone and diminished scales; incorporate exotic scales such as Hungarian major and Gypsy minor; and much more!
_____00695563 Book/CD Pack....................................$14.95

FOR MORE INFORMATION, SEE YOUR LOCAL MUSIC DEALER,
OR WRITE TO:

HAL•LEONARD®
CORPORATION
7777 W. BLUEMOUND RD. P.O. BOX 13819 MILWAUKEE, WI 53213

Visit Hal Leonard Online at
www.halleonard.com

PRICES, CONTENTS AND AVAILABILITY
SUBJECT TO CHANGE WITHOUT NOTICE.

7-STRING GUITAR
AN ALL-PURPOSE REFERENCE FOR NAVIGATING YOUR FRETBOARD
• *by Andy Martin*

Introducing *7-String Guitar*, the first-ever method book written especially for seven-stringed instruments. It teaches chords, scales and arpeggios, all as they are adapted for the 7-string guitar. It features helpful fingerboard charts, and riffs & licks in standard notation and tablature to help players expand their sonic range in any style of music. It also includes an introduction by and biography of the author, tips on how to approach the book, a guitar notation legend, and much more!
_____00695508 ....$12.95

TOTAL ROCK GUITAR
A COMPLETE GUIDE TO LEARNING ROCK GUITAR • *by Troy Stetina*

Total Rock Guitar is a unique and comprehensive source for learning rock guitar, designed to develop both lead and rhythm playing. This book/CD pack covers: getting a tone that rocks; open chords, power chords and barre chords; riffs, scales and licks; string bending, strumming, palm muting, harmonics and alternate picking; all rock styles; and much more. The examples in the book are in standard notation with chord grids and tablature, and the CD includes full-band backing for all 22 songs.
_____00695246 Book/CD Pack.................................$17.95

THE GUITAR F/X COOKBOOK
• *by Chris Amelar*

The ultimate source for guitar tricks, effects, and other unorthodox techniques. This book demonstrates and explains 45 incredible guitar sounds using common stomp boxes and a few unique techniques, including: pick scraping, police siren, ghost slide, church bell, jaw harp, delay swells, looping, monkey's scream, cat's meow, race car, pickup tapping, and much more.
_____00695080 Book/CD Pack.................................$14.95

BLUES YOU CAN USE
• *by John Ganapes*

A comprehensive source designed to help guitarists develop both lead and rhythm playing. Covers: Texas, Delta, R&B, early rock and roll, gospel, blues/rock and more. Includes 21 complete solos; chord progressions and riffs; turnarounds; moveable scales and more. CD features leads and full band backing.
_____00695007 Book/CD Pack.................................$19.95

JAZZ RHYTHM GUITAR
THE COMPLETE GUIDE • *by Jack Grassel*

This book/CD pack by award-winning guitarist and distinguished teacher Jack Grassel will help rhythm guitarists better understand: chord symbols and voicings; comping styles and patterns; equipment, accessories and set-up; the fingerboard; chord theory; and much more. The accompanying CD includes 74 full-band tracks.
_____00695654 Book/CD Pack.................................$19.95